Life in the Spirit
and Mary

CHRISTOPHER O DONNELL, O.Carm.

Michael Glazier, Inc.
Wilmington, Delaware

Second Printing 1988.

First published in 1981 by Michael Glazier, Inc., 1935 West Fourth Street, Wilmington, Delaware 19805.

Distributed outside the U.S., Canada, Australia and the Philippines by Dominican Publications, St. Saviour's, Dublin 1, Ireland

Library of Congress Catalog Card Number: 81-82301
International Standard Book Number: 0-89453-261-8

Cover design by Pat Harris

Printed in the United States of America.

Acknowledgments

Roman Mass texts are from *The Roman Missal,* Liturgical Press and Talbot Press, Dublin, Ireland, and Wm. Collins & Co., Ltd., London-Glasgow, © The International Committee on English in the Liturgy, Inc.

Roman Office texts are from *The Divine Office,* Wm. Collins & Co., Ltd., London-Glasgow, E.J. Dwyer, Sydney, Australia, and Talbot Press, Dublin, ©The Hierarchies of Australia, England and Wales, and Ireland, 1974.

Second Vatican Council texts are from *Vatican II. The Conciliar and Postconciliar Documents,* Dominican Publications and Talbot Press, Dublin, ©Costello Publishing Co., Inc., and Austin Flannery, O.P., 1975.

Biblical texts are from the *Revised Standard Version,* ©Division of Christian Education of the National Council of Churches of Christ in the United States of America.

Liturgical texts of the Eastern Orthodox churches are from Archbishop Joseph Raya and Baron J. de Vinck, *Byzantine Daily Worship,* Alleluia Press, Allendale, New Jersey, U.S.A., and Combermere, Ontario, Canada, 1969; Mother Mary and Archimandrite Kallistos Ware, *The Festal Menaion,* Faber & Faber, London, 1969; *The Divine Liturgies of John Chrysostom, Basil the Great, and that of the Presanctified,* J.N.W.B. Robertson, ed., David Nutt, London, 1894.

My gratitude to Father Paul Lennon, O. Carm., and Sister Helena O'Donoghue, who read the manuscript and made helpful improvements.

Dedicated to
Our Lady of Knock

Contents

Introduction

THERE ARE SIGNS that the church is entering a new era of marian theology and devotion. Inevitably there will be important consequences for that major renewal movement in the church called "charismatic." It is a third phase of marian devotion in the lifetime of many living Catholics, after the two previous periods—namely, before and after the Second Vatican Council (1962–65), a period of great exuberance followed by a period of decline.

In the 1930s and through the 1950s we experienced what is often called the "marian movement," which reached its climax during the pontificate of Pius XII. It was a time of many devotions, of crusades, of copious theological and devotional literature and of much enthusiasm. This movement continuously gained momentum from the second quarter of the century and reached a high point in the definition of the assumption of Mary during the Holy Year of 1950. There followed the Marian Year (1954), but by then the marian movement was already beginning to decline.

The Second Vatican Council was the first ecumenical council to speak directly about Mary, though she was indirectly mentioned in many other councils, especially in the christological definition of the Council of Ephesus, which declared her to be the mother of God (A.D.431). In addition to the splendid eighth chapter of the Second Vatican Council's major document, the *Constitution on the Church*, Mary is mentioned in eleven other conciliar texts. Yet the period after this council seemed to usher in a decline in devotion to her. In some ways the extent of this decline may have been exaggerated. Nonetheless, for many Catholics the role of Mary in the life of the church and in their own spirituality was quite changed.

There are several reasons for the cooling of piety and the altered role of the Virgin Mary. The energies of the post-Vatican II church were largely directed to institutional renewal and liturgical reform, neither of which was likely to foster devotions to or doctrinal studies on Mary. We had to wait for about ten years after the council before a revitalization and rethinking on the role of Mary in Catholic life appeared in official documents of the church. The fine pastoral of the American bishops, *Behold Your Mother. Woman of Faith* (1973), and the apostolic exhortation of Pope Paul VI, *To Honor Mary (Marialis Cultus)*, the following year, were to set a new tone in magisterial statements about Mary. Each was scriptural in orientation, rooted in tradition and sought to develop the thought of the Second Vatican Council in the troubled decade that followed it. They still provide a valuable direction for preachers, theologians and the people of God at prayer.

After the council there was another development—namely, the birth of charismatic renewal in the Catholic Church. Though previously found in other churches, the first major incidence of pentecostal-type activity by Roman Catholics occurred in 1967 among students and staff of Duquesne University and shortly afterward at Notre Dame. Within a few years it would be worldwide. At first, it was called Catholic pentecostalism or neo-pentecostalism, but very soon became more generally known as charismatic renewal or spiritual renewal. The name is not without difficulties, but it is now so widespread that it is probably pointless to seek to change it. It is an adequate name provided we remember that it is not the only renewal movement in the church, and not the only charismatic movement.

The change in terminology from pentecostalism to charismatic renewal is not accidental. There was a deliberate effort to avoid confusion with classical pentecostal churches, such as the Assembly of God, Elim Pentecostals. Even more significantly there quickly emerged a realization that what was happening in the church was no ephemeral phenomenon, no mere prayer movement, but rather a major instrument for the renewal of the whole church. That is still the conviction of the movement's most articulate writers and speakers.

From the beginning charismatic renewal has been interdenominational: public meetings are open to all Christians. For many Catholics charismatic prayer meetings were the first true faith-encounter with other Christians, if we discount for the moment Unity Week celebrations, which often tended to be very formal and even stylized. In meetings for spontaneous prayer, Scripture-sharing, praise or instruction, it is inevitable that some doctrinal questions surface. And not all those involved in charismatic renewal are expert ecumenists.

At times the doctrinal questions were shirked. Silence was the easiest solution and the one most often taken. There are in fact only three approaches one can adopt in an interdenominational faith-sharing.

The first is to speak in such a way as to be fully acceptable to all present. This is extremely difficult and will require adequate theological training in order to do it successfully where doctrinal matters are involved. It has the serious disadvantage of inevitably ending up with a reduction to what is agreeable to all. This effectively prevents the sharing of the positive riches of each faith community. The things in which we differ are not all errors to be rejected: they are often unrenewed riches that we must retain and purify in order to share with our fellow Christians.

The second possibility is that of speaking with simplicity according to one's own faith. This may appear to be divisive, but if it is not triumphalistic or abrasive it will in the long term be the only fruitful approach.

The third possibility is, as we have already noted, silence. This will fail on more than one account. It offends against the cardinal ecumenical principle that we must speak the truth in love (see Eph. 4:15). It creates barriers to faith-sharing: a vague awareness of taboo topics militates strongly against the spontaneity and openness that characterize prayer meetings.

This book is ecumenical in intent. It is a presentation of how one Roman Catholic involved in charismatic renewal sees Mary as a model. If it leads other Christians to reflect on Mary in the light of their own traditions, it will have made a modest contribution to unity. It might also show something of the great riches of the authentic scriptural teaching on Mary. Such biblical reflection should make a contribution to ecumenical dialogue.

The ecumenical thrust of this book lies primarily in its being addressed to Roman Catholics. Inasmuch as charismatic renewal seeks to be a renewal of the whole church, it would seem natural that it assist in the renewal of mariology. Church renewal is an ecumenical task (see Vatican II: *Ecumenism*, 6). It is a more profound work for Christian unity than is dialogue or even cooperation. Dialogue retains importance: we need to learn the insights of different traditions about Mary. In the faith context of the charismatic, group-sharing about the Mother of God is particularly effective. The present work arises from the charismatic renewal and seeks to present the renewed mariology that has emerged from Vatican II and recent scriptural scholarship. It invites Catholics to examine those "old things and new" (See Luke 5:36–39) that are to be found in the living tradition of the people of God.

The first decade of charismatic renewal found little place for Mary, though there were occasional articles and pamphlets such as those by Rosage (1973) and Pfaller-Alberts (1973). With the publication of Cardinal Suenens' book *A New Pentecost* (1974), with a fine chapter on "Mary and the Holy Spirit," and the major charismatic conferences at Lourdes from 1976 onward, there is clearly a changed climate. The eminent mariologist Canon René Laurentin addressed the International Charismatic Conference in Dublin (1978) and has written several articles on Mary and charismatic renewal as well as a chapter "Mary, Model of the Charismatic" in his book *Catholic Pentecostalism* (1977).

In many places charismatic renewal has entered a third stage of development. The first stage was that of *inception.* The movement was then largely peripheral to the life of the church. It was misunderstood and treated with suspicion and even fear. There followed a point of *acceptance.* Pope Paul VI, after some hesitation in 1973, spoke warmly of the renewal in 1975. Bishops became involved or supportive; theologians judged it authentic; clergy, religious and laity became involved in ever greater numbers. Charismatic renewal became "respectable" and was seen to be an authentic expression of Christian life. Where the movement is most mature it has reached a third phase—namely, *integration.* The challenge to charismatic renewal is to face issues such as its relation to the sacramental life of the church, to church institutions, to ecumenism, to social engagement. This promises to be a long and difficult task.

One such concern is clearly to find a rightful place for Mary in an authentic charismatic renewal. One finds occasionally a tendency to overemphasize marian piety at prayer meetings or the idea that marian devotions should take a central focus at charismatic meetings. Those who feel that Mary has been neglected often introduce a marian dimension in an insensitive way. The mere recitation of marian prayers will not be enough to renew and deepen devotion to Mary or to draw our non-Roman brothers and sisters to appreciate the riches we have in the church. Pope Paul VI, indeed, noted in *Marialis Cultus* the danger of reliance on merely external practices in place of serious commitment (n. 38).

Furthermore, when seeking a well-founded presence of Mary in charismatic renewal, we have to be alert to the danger of distorting renewal itself, and especially the prayer meeting. The charismatic renewal prayer meeting is central to the movement. It is a vital element, strongly evangelical, drawing more and more persons to a fresh acceptance of Jesus as Lord and Savior. Again, it is supportive of the conversion that takes place. It is the place where persons come into further healing, where they are instructed, where they learn to pray, where they become aware of the need to live out in practical situations their new commitment to God.

But the prayer meeting is not one's total religious experience. It does not supply all, or even the major needs of a Roman Catholic. Strengthed and sustained by the prayer meeting, I need daily personal prayer, Scripture reading, the sacramental life of the church, especially the Eucharist and the sacrament of reconciliation. I cannot expect to find all these emphasized at a prayer meeting. Likewise I do not expect my full devotion to Mary to find expression at a charismatic meeting.

Nonetheless an authentic role for Mary must be found. If charismatic renewal is to be of the church, if it is to be truly a renewal of the church, it must have Mary as its model. The Second Vatican Council called her a type of the church (*Church*, 63). The church is to turn its eyes to Mary "who shines forth to the whole community of the elect as the model of virtues" (*Church*, 65). We need to see her as the flawless model of all that charismatic renewal hopes to be and seeks to achieve (see Vatican II, *Liturgy*, 103). We are to be brought to the heart of the human and divine dimensions of the mystery of redemption, penetrating with her into the deepest rhythm of the church's life (see Pope John Paul II, Encyclical *Redemptor Hominis* [1979], n. 22).

Though not totally set off from each other, there are three concerns at this time. We have to see Mary as a model for charismatic renewal. Secondly, we have to give Mary due honor in charismatic meetings in a way that is authentically Catholic but ecumenically sensitive. Thirdly, we are to see what new insights the charismatic renewal can bring to marian devotion.

To achieve such aims there are undoubtedly several approaches that might be taken. The approach in this present work is to examine charismatic renewal as it appears in the second decade of its existence in the Catholic Church, and especially to consider its particular spirituality. In subsequent chapters there will be a study of Mary in the New Testament, which will be related to central features of charismatic renewal. Mary will be seen to be a model for the movement in each instance. With the help of some references to the Fathers of the Church and to the liturgy of the East and West, it will appear that the picture of the mother of God thus presented has profound roots in the living tradition of the church.

Chapter I

The Spirituality
of Charismatic Renewal

BEFORE WE CAN BEGIN to study Mary in relation to charismatic renewal, it is necessary to develop some understanding of what the movement is. What is most obvious about a group may not be what is most significant. What strikes one most in a hospital is perhaps the number of persons who wear white, but much more important are the skill and dedication of the staff. Uniforms, or for that matter religious habits, can have a role to play—they signify unity, they help identification—but they are of secondary importance compared with the morale, work and aims of the organization.

What is most conspicuous about charismatic renewal is perhaps the way persons behave at prayer meetings—spontaneous praise, the gift of tongues, uplifted hands. But these are not the essentials of renewal; they are decidedly secondary elements though not without their own importance. We need to get to the heart of charismatic renewal and this we can do best by seeking to grasp its spirituality. The concept of a "spirituality" is not, however, without its difficulties.

There have been many spiritualities in the history of the church, indeed even from New Testament times. The mystery of Christ is one, with unfathomable riches (see Eph. 3:8). A spirituality is a particular ordering of various elements of the mystery of Christ. There will always be central elements common to every spirituality that is authentically Christian. But various spiritualities emphasize one or another quality or dimension of Christ's teaching and life, not indeed to the exclusion of others, but rather as a heightened awareness of some particular features. For example, prayer, a spirit of poverty, trust in God, and simplicity are all gospel values. Any life that is genuinely Christian will have these in evidence. But contemplative institutes stress the importance of prayer; the Franciscan families stress poverty; the writings of de Caussade and Francis de Sales emphasize trust in God and simplicity, respectively.

In the New Testament itself we can point not only to differing theologies but also to differing spiritualities. Thus, it is well known that St. Luke has a major interest in poverty, prayer, the Holy Spirit and his gifts. Johannine spirituality stresses personal faith in Jesus, the glory of the crucified and risen Son of God and fraternal love. These particular points of interest of the two sacred writers are not peculiar to them, but there is more insistence by them on a particular set of values.

Furthermore we find a distinctive spirituality in each of the great religious families, such as the Benedictines and Franciscans. But even in a specific religious institute we will find individuals who are, for example, clearly Franciscan, yet whose way to God may center more on the Eucharist, on Mary or on the Sacred Heart than that of others of the same community. In the life of lay persons or religious we can usually detect some particular focus, some particular ordering of religious truths and practices, that will identify their special approach to the one mystery of Christ. We can note varying spiritualities across denominational boundaries. Thus, Methodist piety is quite clearly distinct from the piety of the Orthodox churches of the East.

Charismatic renewal has its own particular spirituality, its characteristic interests, an identifiable structuring of major religious truths. Attendance at meetings of the movement, faith-sharing with those involved in it, are ways of encountering its spirituality. Certain themes seem to dominate, especially God's love, conversion, openness to God's will, the gifts of the Spirit.

Charismatic renewal is not so much pneumatological as christological—that is to say, it is concerned less with the Holy Spirit and his gifts than with the most primitive of all creeds, "Jesus is Lord" (1 Cor. 12:3). This first credal statement is, of course, trinitarian: it is to the glory of God the Father (see Phil. 2:11) and no one can say "Jesus is Lord" except through the power of the Spirit (1 Cor. 12:3, cf. 1 John 4:2). We find this trinitarian emphasis expanded in the third eucharistic prayer of the Latin Church:

> Father, you are holy indeed and all creation rightly gives you praise. All life, all holiness comes from you through your Son, Jesus Christ our Lord, by the working of the Holy Spirit.

Our lives are directed to the Father, but in the way we pray in the liturgy:

> through our Lord Jesus Christ, your Son, who lives and reigns with you and the Holy Spirit, one God, for ever and ever.

As we grow toward God we develop in our prayer the different relationship we have to each Person of the Trinity: our prayer will not be the same in addressing God as loving Father, God as redeeming Son, God as life-giving Spirit. Though centered on the truth "Jesus is Lord," charismatic renewal is pervasively trinitarian in its hymns, spontaneous prayer and praise, as well as in its scriptural reflections. Thus, its inmost core shows what is common to every Christian manifestation: love of the triune God lived out in a trinitarian life.

Central to charismatic renewal is what is usually called "baptism in the Holy Spirit," the "outpouring of the Holy Spirit" or some similar expression indicative of a conversion experience, which may be sudden or gradual, dramatic or quiet and almost imperceptible. It marks a new stage in spiritual growth. It is not so much the achievement of a degree of Christian perfection as a fresh beginning in which individuals are willing to allow Jesus to be Lord in their lives in a more profound way. It is not a new sacrament but a sending of the Holy Spirit. The early church received a fresh outpouring of the Spirit to enable it to proclaim the gospel with confidence some time after the initial pentecost, as we read:

> and the place in which they were gathered was shaken and they were all filled with the Holy Spirit and spoke the word of God with boldness (Acts 4:31).

Baptism in the Holy Spirit, so called because the word "baptize" means "to plunge into" (see Mark 10:38–39; Luke 12:50), is by no means exclusive to charismatic renewal. Other Christians experience it as a moment of grace given perhaps at a retreat, at religious profession, at ordination, at marriage, or even quite unexpectedly. Other Christian traditions refer to the same reality as "second blessing," "spiritual awakening," "being a born-again Christian."

Seminars on Life in the Spirit

What is characteristic of the charismatic renewal is not only the central place held by this conversion experience, but also the careful preparation that normally precedes it, as well as the expectation that any willing believer may receive it. It should be a normal fact of Christian life, though the circumstances of its actuation and the form it takes will vary. Concomitant with it, or subsequent to it, will usually be the reception of gifts of the Holy Spirit and spiritual healing. So important is this experience that persons are prepared for it by a six-to-eight-week course in basic Christianity called the Life in the Spirit Seminar. This extended retreat is geared toward full adult commitment and its structure gives the key to the spirituality of charismatic renewal.

Each week is devoted to the prayerful consideration of a particular topic. The first week is devoted to the basic religious truth, "God loves me." It develops the text in the First Letter of John:

> In this is love, not that we loved God but that he loved us and sent his Son to be the expiation for our sins (4:10).

A similar text is found in Romans 5:5: "God's love has been poured into our hearts through the Holy Spirit who has been given to us." The fundamental truth of God's personal love for each one of us is a necessary foundation for any spiritual growth. Whether a person is enmeshed in sin or growing in higher states of prayer, it will be a necessary support for advancement.

The second week reflects on the truth that "God saves." This is a second fundamental truth. We stand in the uneasy situation of being continually tempted to forms of despair or presumption. Our weakness can depress us so that we do not really believe in the possibility of change, of real freedom from sin and failure. We need then to be continually reminded that God saves us. The opposite temptation is to a kind of presumption that would lead us to think that we could grow spiritually through our own efforts. This is akin to the the most human and the most insidious of all heresies, Pelagianism, which exaggerates human effort and free will.

As a heretical movement Pelagianism belongs to the fifth century, but it reflects a deep-rooted tendency in all of us. St. Augustine (d. 430) became the champion of orthodoxy: time and time again he insisted that human effort without grace can accomplish nothing in the spiritual life. The sinner is helpless before receiving the healing grace of Christ. In other words, it is God who saves. We must indeed cooperate, but it is in God's work that we share. The path to full rejection of every trace of Pelagianism—that is, to complete and joyful acceptance of God's gift of salvation—is difficult for most. Often we have to experience failure, to realize many times the weakness of good resolutions, before we are prepared to "let go and let God."

The remaining stages of the Life in the Spirit Seminar are devoted to the consideration of such topics as the new life that God offers, baptism in the Holy Spirit, his gifts, spiritual growth. Again the emphasis is on what God does; we are receptive of and cooperative with what God does in us.

We can consider what takes place in the seminars from either a negative or a positive viewpoint. In the early stages of spiritual growth persons may think more of freedom than of new life. They will readily be drawn by the notion of freedom from sin, from guilt, from anxiety, from fear, from self-rejection. And this freedom comes from the gracious love of the Father. But there follow more positive considerations. I am set free from sin and guilt only to live a new life. I enter into the glory and dignity of the children of God. Paul rejoices that those led by the Spirit of God are children of God: the Spirit bears witness with our spirit that we are children of God (see Rom. 8:14, 16). It is through faith in Christ that we are adopted by the Father:

> To all who receive him, who believed in his name, he gave power to become children of God (John 1:12)

The first characteristic, then, of the spirituality of charismatic renewal is that it is centered on Jesus confessed anew as Lord, through baptism in the Holy Spirit—a conversion gift for which we can prepare by allowing God to touch our lives. It is clearly a receptive spirituality: it stresses more what God does than what we do, though our efforts are not unimportant.

Charisms in the Life of the Church

The second mark of the renewal is that it is strongly and explicitly open to the gifts of the Holy Spirit. This aspect is taken up in the middle of the Life in the Spirit Seminar. Because it is here more than anywhere else that we encounter misunderstandings of charismatic renewal, it may be helpful to look somewhat more closely at charisms in the church.

Even a cursory reading of the New Testament will detect the presence of gifts of the Spirit, including some that are quite remarkable. They are given, as Paul says in the Greek phrase, *pros to sympheron* (1 Cor. 12:7), which is perhaps best translated "for profit" rather than more narrowly "for the common good" (*RSV*).

There are several lists of these gifts in the New Testament. In 1 Corinthians 12 we find utterance of wisdom and knowledge, faith, healings, miracles, prophecy, discernment of spirits, tongues and the interpretation of tongues. In Ephesians 4 we note apostles, prophets, evangelists, pastors, teachers in roles of service. Romans 12 gives prophecy, ministry, teaching, exhortation, almsgiving, ruling, doing works of mercy. Other lists occur elsewhere in the New Testament, but it is clear that there is never an attempt to give an exhaustive list of the gifts of the Spirit, who, quite simply, breathes where he will (John 3:8).

Everything we receive from God is a gift. In our present context we are speaking of a *particular type* of gift, one that is distributed by the Spirit to various members of the church (see 1 Cor. 12:11). We are not speaking here about the gifts necessary for personal holiness and salvation — for example, faith, hope, love, graces. The gifts or charisms we are concerned with here are for works within the Body of Christ (see 1 Cor. 12:7).

It is not always clear as we read the New Testament account of gifts whether we are dealing with an office or a charism: is the sacred writer referring to an office in the church or to a gifted person? The two need not be distinct.

There were teachers in the church, many of whom presumably had the charism of teaching with power and insight. Prophets too seemed to be a special class in the church. In other instances, however, it may not be clear. What is quite certain is that the gifts were to be used in an ordered way. Paul lays down quite specific rules for the exercise of charisms (1 Cor. 14).

A charism is a free gift that equips a person to perform some function in the church. Apart from the charism of tongues, perhaps, the function is always a ministry or service in the church. There is in the New Testament a clear refusal to equate holiness and charism. In Corinth there were many who had genuine charisms but were described by Paul as being "puffed up" with pride (see 1 Cor. 4:18–19; 5:2; 8:1; in contrast, see 13:4: "love is not puffed up").

The opening of the First Letter to the Corinthians is very interesting in this context. Paul normally opens his letters with a thanksgiving for the love, faith and hope of the recipient church (e.g., Col. 1; 1 Thess. 1; Phil. 1), but in the case of the Corinthian church he cannot thank God for their love, which is singularly absent, so he contents himself with a profound thanksgiving for the charisms they have received:

> I give thanks to God always for you because of the grace of God which was given you in Christ Jesus, that in every way you were enriched in him with all speech and all knowledge ... so that you are not lacking in any spiritual gift (1 Cor. 1:4-7).

The fact that charisms do not necessarily sanctify and may be used by sinners emerges also in the stern warning of Jesus that those with remarkable gifts may be excluded from the kingdom:

> On that day many will say to me "Lord, Lord, did we not prophesy in your name, and cast out demons in your name, and do many mighty works in your name?"

And then I will declare to them, "I never knew you;
depart from me, you evildoers" (Matt. 7:22–23).

Hence, though there are undoubtedly many charisms
present in the charismatic renewal, these are not to be confused with holiness. The charisms are good, but "a more
excellent way" is love (1 Cor. 12:31).

There are differing views as to why charisms seemed to
disappear from the church after the first few centuries. Until the Second Vatican Council, the most common opinion
was dispensationalism: the charisms were given at the beginning of the church to help its growth in the particular
difficulties of its origins. But during the Council another
view, put forward strongly by Cardinal Suenens, was to
triumph—namely, that the charisms belong to the very
nature of the church and will be found throughout its life
and activity. The final text of the council reads:

> It is not only through the sacraments and the ministra-
> tions of the church that the Holy Spirit makes holy the
> people, leads them and enriches them with his virtues.
> Allotting his gifts according as he wills (1 Cor. 12:11), he
> also distributes special graces among the faithful of
> every rank. By these gifts he makes them fit and ready
> to undertake various tasks and offices for the renewal
> and building up of the church, as it is written, "the
> manifestation of the Spirit is given to everyone for profit"
> (1 Cor. 12:7). Whether these charisms be very
> remarkable or more simply and widely diffused, they
> are to be received with thanksgiving and consolation
> since they are fitting and useful for the needs of the
> church (*Church*, 12).

The Council makes a distinction between extraordinary
and ordinary charisms. This terminology, however, is not
biblical, and indeed the history of the church, particularly
since the council itself, shows that many gifts that might be
called "extraordinary" are very common indeed.

The reason for the present abundance of charisms lies primarily in the sovereign will of God. A condition that makes the reception of charisms possible is expectancy. At the present time there is a new eagerness to receive charisms (see 1 Cor. 12:31; 14:1, 12). A widespread openness to charisms has been lacking in the church for many centuries, perhaps from the time of Montanism in the Third century, which led to a deep distrust of the unusual, of emotion, of enthusiasm. Some charisms were always expected, such as the grace of office for those bearing authority in the church, but on the whole the faithful tended to associate remarkable charisms with saints. But we have seen that charism does not imply holiness in the recipient. The charismatic renewal has a profound sense of expectancy with regard to charisms: they are presumed to be part of the normal Christian life of the community, and in fact this is borne out by the experience of those involved in the renewal. Later we shall see an authentic marian approach to charisms.

Conversion and Community

The third major thrust of the spirituality of charismatic renewal is that it is turned toward rejuvenation and community. The individual encounters the charismatic renewal usually at a prayer meeting or a conference. There follows a conversion experience in which Jesus is recognized in a new way as Lord and Saviour. One or more charismatic gifts may be received or deepened in the person. But the process must not stop there, for inherent in the personal conversion must be an orientation to community, to the renewal of the church. The community dimension takes many forms, but in some way it should express a new concern for the whole church, for ecumenism, for unrenewed structures, as well as solicitude for weak and traumatized individuals in the community.

Some communities have arisen within the charismatic renewal with strong bonds between the members; these de-

mand deep commitment on the part of the individuals concerned. The vision these communities have of themselves is
that of being a renewing leaven within the church (see
Matt. 13:33). There are other community manifestations
making lesser demands: they also seek to show, in a different way, how the Spirit empowered the early Christians:

> And they devoted themselves to the apostles' teaching
> and fellowship, to the breaking of bread and prayers
> ... the community of those who believed were of one
> heart and soul ... with great power the apostles gave
> their testimony to the resurrection of the Lord Jesus, and
> great grace was upon them all (Acts 2:42; 4:32–33).

These texts have been the inspiration of countless
religious orders and congregations. They give rise today to
new communities in the rich variety of charismatic rejuvenation.

Charismatic renewal has also in many places profoundly
influenced existing communities such as religious houses,
parishes and church organizations. As their members come
to baptism in the Holy Spirit and experience a range of
charisms, they are renewed in many aspects of their life
and find new potentialities for growth and service.

Even those who do not have the opportunity of association with or membership in a charismatic community can
appreciate the new ability to share and care that is en-
countered in the prayer meeting and other life situations.
These are genuine manifestations of community. The
essential point is that no authentic religious experience can
be merely for the individual alone. It is in the communion
of saints that we grow in holiness.

Mary, Model of Outreach

As we reflect on the spirituality of charismatic renewal,
we look also to Mary. The Second Vatican Council pre-

sented her as the model of everything that the church is to be. It is in its text on the liturgy that we find the most succinct statement on Mary's role in the church and for us:

> In celebrating this annual cycle of the mysteries of Christ, holy church honors the Blessed Mary, mother of God, with a special love. She is inseparably linked with her Son's saving work. In her the church admires and exalts the most excellent fruit of redemption, and joyfully contemplates, as in a faultless image, that which she herself desires and hopes wholly to be (*Liturgy*, 103).

If charismatic renewal is genuinely of the church, then Mary must be the faultless image of all it desires and hopes for. It is also important to remember that it is in celebrating the mysteries of Christ that we are to honor Mary. It is in the very act of proclaiming Jesus to be Lord in our lives that we can come to know her who is inseparably linked with his saving work. Further, we are to show her special love, recognizing that she is truly our mother, and mother of the charismatic renewal.

The charismatic renewal must, therefore, reflect Mary's motherhood. It shares in the ceaseless giving birth to new life that is the Spirit's work. The primary work of the renewal is to bring persons into a new faith in Jesus Christ as Lord and Savior. This conversion is a fresh manifestation of our baptismal calling. Mary's intercession is intimately connected with this, for as Vatican II states:

> Taken up into heaven she did not lay aside this saving office, but by her maternal intercession continues to bring us the gifts of eternal salvation (*Church*, 62).

This work of Mary through her intercession as she pleads continually for her children may be seen as expressed in the saying of St. Augustine:

> She is clearly the mother of the members of Christ . . . she has by her charity joined in bringing about the birth

of believers in the church, who are members of its head (quoted by Vatican II, *Church*, 53).

She cooperates in our spiritual birth. Hence we can understand more profoundly the text of John 3:3:"Unless persons be born anew [or "from above"], they cannot see the kingdom of God." To be born demands a mother. We are continually being born again as children of God. Our identification with Christ whereby we are children of God (see Rom. 8:14-16) is a process of continual growth. Our mother intercedes continually for us so that we may grow into fullness of life in her Son. Thus, for the new life we experience in the charismatic renewal we have Mary as mother.

In our grateful use of charisms we have Mary as model. She received the gift of God (see John 4:10) when the Holy Spirit descended upon her (see Luke 1:35). We are to receive God's gifts in an attitude of faith and trust and we are to use them to bring forth Jesus in ourselves and others.

The charismatic renewal also has Mary as mother of its ceaseless outreach to others. The Second Vatican Council stated that she is "a type of the church in the order of faith, charity and perfect union with God" (*Church*, 63).

Centered on the crucial affirmation that Jesus Christ is Lord, those in the charismatic renewal seek to go beyond what is personal to the wider needs of the church and the world. In this the movement has in Mary a most perfect model in what it is seeking. Pope Paul VI stated that the church and Mary collaborate to give birth to the Mystical Body and he went on to quote the ancient writer, Isaac de Stella: "both of them are mother of Christ, but neither brings forth the whole [body] without the other" (*Marialis Cultus*, 28).

The charismatic renewal is therefore to be marian not merely in the sense of having devotional exercises honoring Mary, but much more profoundly, by having at its heart the attitude of Mary. In the following chapters we shall study the picture of Mary and develop in greater detail what has been outlined in this present chapter.

Chapter II

Mary The Receptive Virgin

THERE IS a short text in the New Testament that is extra-ordinarily rich, even though it may seem to say little at first sight. It occurs in Matthew 13:55 (Mark 6:3), where it is found in the context of a return of Jesus to his own hometown of Nazareth. The villagers are amazed at him, but they do not want to accept him as teacher. They point to his relatives who are well known and remark, "Is not his mother called Mary?" (Matt. 13:55).

The mystery of the incarnation of the Son of God was worked out in secrecy, a secrecy so total that persons in his own hometown never suspected anything out of the or-dinary. The life of the holy family at Nazareth was so con-ventional that others could point to it as a reason to justify disbelief—that man's mother was Mary!

It is possible that there is here also a suggestion that there had been something irregular about the birth of Jesus. Perhaps the villagers are referring to the fact that Mary had a child who was conceived before she and Joseph came to be married, because she returned to her own home after spending three months with Elizabeth (see Luke 1:56). (The retort of the Jews reported in John 8:41 may also be a reference to supposed improbity on the part of Joseph and Mary.)

We cannot be certain that there was not a hint of op-probrium in being Mary's son, or whether it was merely an assertion that anybody born of such an ordinary woman certainly could not be important. At any rate the Nazareth years were part of the self-emptying of the Son of God (see

Phil. 2:7) who became like us in all things but sin (see Heb. 2:17; 4:15). The silence of Nazareth is almost total. We are told of one incident when Jesus was twelve, then nothing except for the simple statement:

> And he went down with them and came to Nazareth, and was obedient to them . . . and Jesus increased in wisdom and in stature, and in favor with God and man (Luke 2:51–52).

We may at times regret that we do not know more about the hidden life, but that is in a subtle way to complain about the word of God. We have been told what God wills us to know. Our task is to contemplate what God has chosen to reveal. In this case it is to reflect on the concealment of the glory of the Son of God in a mystery of silence and ordinariness.

A consideration of the normality of the hidden life of Nazareth can prepare us to enter into the divine plan manifested in Mary, mother of God. It will also bring us to what is very central in the spirituality of the charismatic renewal. Mary is above all else the receptive virgin. She is blessed not so much by what she did but by what she received. A key to the understanding of the mother of God is the line from the Magnificat, "He who is mighty has done great things for me and holy is his name"(Luke 1:49).

To honor Mary is to celebrate God's work in her; it is to praise God whose power has been at work in each of what are usually called the privileges of Mary.

If Protestant theology exalts the principle of "grace alone" (*gratia sola*), there is no more perfect example of it than the immaculate conception. Clearly Mary could have done nothing to earn this grace. It was the absolutely gratuitous love of God for her that kept her free from the first moment of her existence from all trace of original sin.

We can see this mystery in relation either to Christ or to the church. Related to the incarnation, the immaculate conception can be seen as the preparation of a worthy mother for the Son of God: it would be totally inappropriate that the Mother of God should at any time be under the influence of sin. Related to the church, the immaculate conception is a model for the church, which must ever more seek to be sinless. In the Roman rite these two ideas are found combined in the preface of the Mass:

> You allowed no stain of Adam's sin to touch the Virgin Mary. Full of grace, she was to be a worthy mother of your Son, your sign of favor to the church at its beginning, and the promise of its perfection as the bride of Christ, radiant in beauty. Purest of virgins, she was to bring forth your Son, the innocent lamb who takes away our sins. You chose her from all women to be our advocate with you and our pattern of holiness.

The immaculate conception does not make Mary distant from us; on the contrary, she comes closer. Sin dehumanizes. Mary, the sinless one, is most fully human. Similarly, the more sinless we are, the more compassionate we can be. This last may seem paradoxical, but it can be daily verified in practice: the more we sin, the less kind we tend to be toward others who fail. Mary, being without sin, can truly be a compassionate mother in our sinfulness. It is in being totally receptive to God's grace that Mary is most fully our model. If she can receive such a marvelous grace as to be preserved from original, and later actual, sin, we can be healed from our sinfulness through the same mercy.

The divine maternity is again a matter of pure grace. Mary received the gift of her Son. Again she is the receptive virgin.

Her word to the angel at the annunciation is expressed in a special way in the Greek of St. Luke's gospel: it is in the optative mood and can be best translated "Oh, let it be done to me according to your word" (1:38). This is not a passive acceptance, but a joyful desire that the word be fulfilled. The emphasis, nonetheless, is on receiving; Mary leaves herself open to God's action.

In the Latin church there is a strong tradition in calling Mary "ark of the convenant." This has a solid biblical basis. In the Old Testament the place of meeting was covered over with a cloud and filled with the glory of God (see Exod.40:35). Mary is overshadowed by the Holy Spirit (see Luke 1:35). She becomes the new ark of the covenant, the place where God chooses to dwell. She receives the second person of the Trinity. Her maternity shows that fruitfulness is before all else a work of the Spirit. We receive from God before we can bear fruit in his service.

These ideas are echoed in the Sunday Office of the Byzantine church:

> O Virgin, when Gabriel hailed you, at the sound of his voice the Lord of all was conceived in you, and you became a holy temple, foretold by David the just man. Bearing your creator, you became more spacious than heaven. Glory to him who dwelled in you! Glory to him who came forth from you! Glory to him who set us free by being born of you (First Tone of Resurrection).

The perpetual virginity is another gift of grace. Mary is ever-virgin, or as the classic formula has it, she was virgin before, during and after the birth of Christ.

In this she is once more the receptive virgin. The charism of virginity is a gift, freely bestowed by God. Virginity in the Christian sense is no mere absence of sexual activity; on the contrary, it is fruitful love. If persons are not open to *agape*, the special love of Christian revelation which is self-emptying in the service of God and others—they may indeed be pure but they will not be enjoying the charism of celibacy or, more profoundly, virginity.

If we understand virginity to be perpetual and undefiled celibacy, we can then speak directly about the lesser gift of celibacy, knowing that all that is said will apply to virginity also. Celibacy is about loving. Though it does make a person free (see 1 Cor. 7:32–34), its profoundest meaning is not to be sought in this alone. It is for the sake of the kingdom of God (see Matt. 19:12): celibacy seeks a total commitment to the affairs of God, a here-and-now donation of the undivided love that will characterize all in the future kingdom.

Celibacy and poverty are closely allied: celibacy is one way of being poor in order that God may make us rich in unselfish loving. Mary is totally enriched by the love of God and of all humankind, the latter to be given to her as her children.

The liturgy of the Eastern churches continuously celebrates the virginity of Mary. Characteristic is this prayer from the Night Office:

> It is fitting and right to call you blessed, O Theotokos, the ever-blessed and all-blameless one, and the mother of our God. O you, higher in honor than the cherubim and most glorious beyond compare than the seraphim, you gave birth to God the Word in virginity. You are truly mother of God: you do we exalt.

Finally, the assumption is a gift of God. Mary did nothing to merit or earn this grace: it is purely God's favor toward her. The church's meditation on the assumption shows the mystery to be a consoling one: already one of our race is fully redeemed. We are also invited to reflect on the consummation of the divine motherhood. We can see these two notions in the preface of the feast in the Roman Missal:

> The virgin mother of God was taken up into heaven to be the beginning and the pattern of the church in its perfection, and a sign of hope and comfort for your people on their pilgrim way. You would not allow decay to touch her body, for she had given birth to your Son, the Lord of all life, in the glory of the incarnation.

Similar ideas are found in the liturgy of the East—for example, in the Great Vespers of the dormition of the Blessed Virgin (August 15):

> Come, O gathering of those who love to keep the feasts, Come and let us form a choir. Come let us crown the church with songs, as the ark of God goes to her rest. For today is heaven opened wide as it receives the mother of him who cannot be contained. The earth as it yields up the source of life, is robed in blessing and majesty. The hosts of angels present, with the fellowship of the apostles, gaze in great fear at her who bore the cause of life, now that she is translated from life to life. Let us all venerate and implore her: Forget not, O Lady, thy ties of kinship with those who commemorate in faith the feast of thine all-holy dormition. (ascribed to Theophanes)

When we celebrate Mary as receptive virgin we are not suggesting that she was utterly passive. It is a matter of emphasis, of priority. What is the most significant aspect of Mary's life? Is it what she did or what God did in her? Clearly the latter. She did, of course, correspond with what God did; "she conceived in her heart before she conceived in her womb," St. Augustine notes several times (e.g.,*Serm.* 196, *Serm. Denis* 25). Hers was a total response to the grace she was given.

Thus, when we stress Mary's receptivity as being at the heart of her mystery and of her being our model, we are in no sense advocating a quietistic spirituality—that is, one in which the person is merely receptive. The gospels attest to her active response to God's will, but this is in answer to what God had previously done in her. She indeed said "yes," but it was to God's invitation. Her receptivity then is active, open to the Spirit, but the initiative is always with God, the emphasis is on what he does. Again, we can go to St. Augustine for a terse summary: "she brought forth by believing, she conceived by believing" (*Serm.* 215).

Charismatic Renewal and the Receptive Virgin

As we turn to the charismatic renewal we can note that its spirituality is profoundly receptive. With even a slight acquaintance with prayer meetings or with those involved in the renewal, one is likely to be struck by such phrases as "the Lord did....," or "we must be open to the Lord..." Again, the accent on charism points to receptivity, for charism is a freely bestowed gift. But ways of speaking and praying and the gifts of the Spirit themselves, though important, are rather peripheral compared with the heart of the charismatic renewal: baptism in the Holy Spirit. This, as we have previously noted, is a conversion experience in which one accepts anew Jesus as Lord. All Pelagianism or exaggeration of human efforts is rejected, for this is most profoundly a gift of the Spirit. It is not the consummation of holiness, but rather an opening out toward God. It is a "yes" to an initiative that belongs to God.

Baptism in the Holy Spirit always follows or begins a healing process. Healing is an extremely complex notion, because the weaknesses we experience are manifold. What concerns us at this point is primarily the sickness, the distortion of our personality that results from sin.

Our past sins can leave effects on later life. Anger, bitterness, disordered relationships of whatever kind, can lead to a state that is spiritually and psychologically unhealthy, a state in which we are "estranged and hostile in mind" (see Col. 1:21). The sin may well be forgiven, but the effects linger on and they can invade our relationships with God and with other persons. Those in the charismatic renewal are familiar with prayer for inner healing: we submit the damaged areas of our emotions to the Lord that he may touch us and heal even the causes of what disturbs us.

In charismatic renewal we soon learn that God does not will to *cure* all weakness and illness, but he does will to *heal*. To cure would be to take away the problem; to heal can mean to touch us with his love so that we can now deal with the difficulty. We are thus raised up to a new maturity in Christ.

Weaknesses that come from past sinfulness are not the only area that needs healing. We can also inherit weakness from our parents. This too can be healed, especially through the healing sacrament of the anointing of the sick, the sacrament of reconciliation—when the weakness has led us into sin—and the great healing sacrament of the Eucharist. Prayer for healing is common in the charismatic renewal, and is very effective, especially when combined with healing sacraments.

When, from our unhealed state, we look to Mary, we find new grounds for hope. For she is the most perfectly healed one: because she was never touched by sin, she has full integrity of emotions, of mind and body. Her immaculate conception and her sinlessness ensured that her Son would be born free from any negative influence arising from procreation. Mary is the model of fully healed humanity: we are to receive healing from the same Lord who preserved his mother free from all taint. Our hope is to be more and more patterned on our mother.

Of all gifts, that of the reception of healing is perhaps the most passive: we do nothing to earn or accomplish healing; it is pure gift. We have only to come to the Lord, as Isaiah calls to us:

> Everyone who thirsts, come to the waters; and they who have no money, come buy and eat! Come, buy wine and milk without money and without cost (55:1).

Our role is to will the removal of blockages to healing, and even this is the result of grace. The restoration or healing that we need will be continuous: we can always become more conformed to our mother. This lifelong emergence to fullness of growth and development will perhaps be completed only in the compassionate healing that is purgatory. In the meanwhile we will be receiving salvation continually:

> For by grace you have been saved through faith. It is the gift of God—not because of works, lest anyone should boast. For we are his workmanship, created in Christ

Jesus for good works, which God prepared beforehand, that we should walk in them (Eph. 2:8–10).

Salvation will never be an acquired or sure possession but always what we shall be straining toward.

Mary's divine maternity is no less a model for charismatic renewal. As we seek personal renewal and the renewal of the church we recognize that it is not something that we accomplish, but what God accomplishes in us and through us. We have to echo Mary's cry, "Oh, let it be done unto me according to thy word" (Luke 1:38) and thus allow God to use us to bear fruit in his church.

We know that Mary is a mother to us in the order of grace (Vatican II:Church,61) so that our fruitfulness is both a sharing in her universal maternity and at the same time a deeper recognition of her as our mother. That is to say, we reflect Mary when we bring Jesus her Son to those who do not yet have him in fullness. By the same token, we need her motherly care so that we can do this.

Mary fulfilled the picture of motherhood given by Jesus:

> When a woman is in travail she has sorrow, because her hour has come; but when she is delivered of the child, she no longer remembers the anguish, for joy that a child is born into the world (John 16:21).

She came to be mother of the whole Christ at the foot of the cross. Because she had been faithful in keeping the word of God (Luke 11:28), she receives a new vocation to be mother of all humankind.

When the sons of Zebedee asked for high places in the kingdom, Jesus asked them if they were able to drink the cup that he was to drink (Mark 10:35–38). Mary drank the cup of pain on Calvary when she saw her Son put to death with extreme cruelty. She suffered also as a daughter of Sion in seeing her people reject God's plan for them. But as her Son's "hour" was passion and glorification (see John 2:3; 8:20; 17:1), so her hour, in travail, was perfect conformity with the will of the Father and trust in him. As the church is being born on Calvary, Mary receives the beloved disciple as son, and through him all humankind.

Charismatic renewal, in looking to Mary as a model, will see that tribulation is part of what it means to be a follower of her Son. This was foretold in the Old Testament:

> My son, if you come forward to serve the Lord, prepare yourself for temptation. Set your heart right and be steadfast, and do not be hasty in time of calamity. Cleave to him and do not depart, that you may be honored at the end of your life. Accept whatever is brought upon you, and in changes that humble you be patient. Trust in him and he will help you (Sir. 2:1–6).

In the New Testament there is a more profound understanding of tribulation: although it is inevitable, it can bring joy. Thus Paul speaks in Romans of a whole process of up-building:

> More than that, we rejoice in our sufferings, knowing that suffering produces endurance, and endurance produces character, and character produces hope, and hope does not disappoint us, because God's love has been poured into our hearts through the Holy Spirit who has been given to us (5:3–5).

Thus, rather than think that the early exhilaration of the time following the baptism in the Holy Spirit is "normal," we need to be prepared for difficulty as being the common lot of the Christian. Mary will be for us a model of steadfastness.

We have considered virginity as love in action, a love of God and others that diffuses itself and cannot be restricted within the family circle. Whatever our state, married or single, we need to look to Mary's total dedication to God and seek to reflect it according to our circumstances. But human love is always fragile. It can so easily be tainted with selfishness or egotism. We need to receive a love that will allow us to love in return. This demands a new creation (see Gal. 6:15; 2 Cor. 5:17).

In a profound text Paul speaks of the lighting up of our hearts as a new creative act by God:

> For it is the God who said, "let light shine out of darkness," who has shone in our hearts to give the light of the knowledge of the glory of God in the face of Christ (2 Cor. 4:6).

In the Bible the heart stands for the core of our being, the center of our existence. We all know how fickle this is (see Jer. 17:9). God's promise in the Old Testament was the removal of the former heart (Ezek. 36:25) and the implanting of his law in our hearts (Jer. 31:33). Just as the Spirit hovered over the abyss at the beginning (Gen. 1:2), so God's power overshadows our weakness (2 Cor. 12:9) and he performs a great act of re-creation in our disordered hearts: "let there be light." We can now enter into the knowledge of the glory of God. "Knowledge" is meant here in the strong biblical sense of *experiencing* this glory. The glory in the face of Christ is both cross and resurrection. Hence the creative word of God brings us into a special relationship with the suffering and risen Christ. It is now possible to love in a way that is unselfish.

We can imitate the God-centered and other-centered virginal love of Mary. Baptism in the Spirit is leading us all the time toward a transformation of our entire being. We have the firstfruits of the Spirit (see Rom. 8:23; 2 Cor. 1:22). We are, as it were, in travail until our redemption is fully accomplished, as we wait in patience for what we do not yet have (see Rom. 8:22–25). Meanwhile Mary, the assumed one, is the model of what we are to be. Just as her sinlessness is a pattern for us—we have to become ever more sinless and healed—so too the assumption points to a glory that is gradually to be revealed in our mortal bodies.

Mary and the Church

A common theme in the Fathers of the Church is the comparison between the church and Mary. This occurs in various forms, often aligned to the New Eve theology that we shall examine later. It can be found in a very summary form in St. Isidore of Spain:

> Mary signifies the church for the latter is espoused to Christ, and she as a virgin conceived us of the Holy Spirit, and virginally brought us forth (*Allegories*,139).

Each of the marian mysteries that shows her as the receptive virgin points to differing aspects of baptism in the Holy Spirit. Mary remains the flawless model of all we hope to be (Vatican II: *Liturgy*, 103). There are, however, two ways of looking at a model, at something better than what we have or are. A first, superficial attitude might be one of regret at the lack of the particular good in question. But the more mature approach is to allow the ideal to attract us. We may not yet have arrived at the particular state—for example, sinlessness—but we rely on the power of God who one day will make us whole and without spot or wrinkle (Eph. 5:27). All the time we are encouraged by the image of Mary who has already achieved what we long for.

Growth in the spiritual life resembles aesthetics, the appreciation of the beautiful. It is not so much a matter of obeying laws, correcting faults, and striving after spiritual perfection, as it is of allowing ourselves to be drawn by the beauty of God. We can never capture beauty, make it exclusively our own. It remains outside us, but attracts us, moves us toward it. This is at the heart of the *Song of Songs* in the Old Testament, a story of love's desire. In this aesthetic context Mary appears as a figure of repose and tranquility. We can look at her without being threatened by our own inadequacy. She points to what can be accomplished by the grace of Christ. Where she is, we are called to be. That is why the celebration of Mary's liturgical feasts has a holiday quality for the people of God. The word of God in the liturgy continually calls us to repentance, to carry the cross, to live uprightly. But the marian feasts are to be enjoyed for their own sake. We can be glad at them and seek nothing further.

Something of the same emerges when we study the spirituality of Eastern icons. These sacred paintings are not so much a reminder of the saint—in our case, Mary— as a focus or encounter between the person who venerates the icon and the one venerated. As I pray before an icon of the Blessed Virgin I allow her to look at me through the quasi-sacramental image, and at the same time I feel drawn toward her who remains still veiled behind the icon. The holy icon is a meeting place between heaven and earth. It can lead to prayer of petition, of sorrow for sin, but most often it should lead to a quiet contemplative prayer echoing the cry of Peter, "it is well that we are here" (Matt. 17:4).

We began with a consideration of the ordinariness of Mary. Despite her glory in the eyes of God, to the people of Nazareth she was the carpenter's wife. Rather than making fanciful pictures of the life of Mary, it is perhaps best to stand amazed at this picture of emptying, of poverty. We know of the repeated warnings of Jesus against riches. Wealth is not evil, but it can turn our hearts away from God and lead us into a proud self-sufficiency (see Luke 12:16–21). Evangelical poverty has us put our riches in God. The Second Vatican Council teaches that Mary "stands out among the poor and humble of the Lord who confidently hope for and receive salvation from him" (Church,55). Her riches were totally in God.

In the charismatic renewal we learn that God is strong, that he is trustworthy and faithful:

I sing thy praise
and give thanks to thy holy name for thy steadfast love
   and faithfulness. . . .

On the day I called thou didst answer me. . . .
Though I walk in the midst of trouble, thou dost
    preserve my life. . . .
The Lord will fulfil his purpose for me;
thy steadfast love endures forever (Ps. 138).

But though he is our rock, our fortress, our deliverer
(Ps. 18:2), we have to learn the lesson of our own poverty.
The critical time follows upon the baptism in the Holy
Spirit when, after several months or longer, the journey
toward God, which seemed so easy, is so no longer. Just as
the Lord after his baptism was led into the desert to be
tempted by the devil (see Luke 4:1-2), so we are usually led
in dark ways. Prayer that was effortless now becomes dry
and dull. The zest for serving God seems to have gone. Sinful habits that we thought cured now return. Areas that
seemed healed seem to be as they were before we en-
countered the Lord in the charismatic renewal. All seems
pallid. We have turned our back on so many things in
order to seek God, and now we appear to have lost him
too.
    This is a time of testing; it may last months or even
years. It is a critical period during which many turn back
and we have the phenomenon of "lapsed charismatics." It
is now that the hidden life of Mary and Joseph together
with Jesus can become especially meaningful. We are told
of only one supernatural revelation in the case of Mary.
"And the angel departed from her" clearly rounds off the
story of the annunciation: the angel comes and then goes
(Luke 1:26, 38). But it is also the end of revelations for
Mary. It was not from angels but from shepherds—known
at the time for their ignorance and dishonesty— that Mary
learned of the heavenly message at Bethlehem concerning
her Son (Luke 2:16-19).
    In the trials of growth in the Spirit the sheer ordinariness
of Mary's home at Nazareth is a challenge and a consolation. There is need to do good works so that our light may
shine and others may give glory to the Father (Matt.

5:14–16), but we must also do good in ways that are un-
noticed (Matt. 6:2–6). Beyond this is the invitation to be
empty, hidden, perhaps misunderstood so that still greater
glory may be given to God, as we read in the life of St.
Paul:

> We are treated as imposters and yet are true; as
> unknown and yet well known; as dying, and behold, we
> live; as punished, and yet not killed; as sorrowful, yet
> always rejoicing; as poor, yet making many rich; as
> having nothing, and yet possessing everything (2 Cor.
> 6:8–10).

This is also a time of temptation by the evil one. We can
be confident in the protection of the woman whose seed
crushed the head of the serpent (see Gen. 3:15). This victory over evil is often celebrated in the liturgy, especially
of the East. Thus from the Matins of the feast of the annunciation in the Byzantine rite:

> Today all creation rejoices, for the archangel says unto
> thee, "Hail! Blessed art thou, O pure and holy, undefiled
> and spotless." Today the proud insolence of the serpent
> is brought low, for the fetters of the curse laid on our
> forefathers are loosened. Therefore with all the world
> we cry aloud to thee: Hail, thou who art full of grace.

Growth in the Spirit is the call to bring our ordinary
lives into the sphere of God. If those lives were continually
suffused with light, they would not be ordinary. We are
called to be Marylike in not being noticed by those around
us so that we may be Christlike in loving them. To achieve
this we need to share in the victory of Christ and his
mother over evil.

The liturgy often reflects on this mystery of weakness
and strength, the ordinary and extraordinary. Some
prayers used in the Roman rite sum up these ideas:

> Father, source of light in every age, the virgin conceived

and bore your Son who is called Wonderful God, Prince of Peace. May her prayer, the gift of a mother's love, be your people's joy through all ages. May her response, born of a humble heart, draw your Spirit to rest on your people (Solemnity of Mary, Mother of God).

But it is above all in the ecstatic poetry of the Eastern liturgy that we are brought into the mystery of weakness and humility. Thus the Matins for the annunciation in the Byzantine rite has this dialogue between Mary and the angel:

Mary: "My mother Eve, accepting the suggestion of the serpent, was banished from divine delight; therefore I fear thy strange salutation, for I take heed lest I slip."
Angel: "I am sent as the envoy of God to disclose to thee the divine will. Why art thou, O undefiled, afraid of me, who rather am afraid of thee? Why, O Lady, dost thou stand in awe of me, who stand in awe of thee?"

The Eastern liturgy loves to dwell on the great paradox of the Lord of the universe being held as a helpless baby; it sings of him who feeds the world being himself nourished by Mary. But the liturgy of both East and West respects the gospel silence about the mysterious time of emptiness and growth in the obscurity of Nazareth.

Always we come back to the receptive virgin: she received God in her womb; she received all else besides. Yet it was in that obscurity that haunts our vision. About the year A.D. 110 the martyr Ignatius wrote in a letter to the church at Ephesus:

From the prince of this world was hidden the virginity of Mary and her childbearing as well as the death of the Lord—three resonant mysteries performed in the silence of God.

And it is in silent contemplation that we leave the virgin still in her glorified state receptive of the vision of God.

Chapter III

Mary and Her Son — Jesus is Lord

"JESUS IS LORD" is the earliest Christian creed. Inasmuch as it is an act of faith, it can be affirmed only through the power of the Holy Spirit. As we study Mary and see her as a model for the charismatic renewal, we find her living out this most central of all Christian beliefs.

The life of Jesus is a progressive revelation of his lordship. From the beginning there were signs that led the disciples to faith — an immature faith, it is true. An example of such initial faith is Peter. He confessed Jesus to be the Messiah (Mark 8:29). However, when Jesus goes on to explain that the Messiah would have to suffer many things, be rejected by the religious authorities and killed, Peter rejects this teaching and rebukes Jesus for speaking in this way (Mark 8:32). The response of Jesus is the sharp "Get behind me, Satan," for Peter was doing the work of Satan in seeking to deflect Jesus from the role of the suffering Messiah (see Luke 4:3–13).

There are many other instances of initial faith in the gospels, such as the recognition of Jesus as a prophet (Luke 7:16) and the first manifestation of his glory at Cana (John 2:11). But it will be only when he is "designated Son of God in power according to the Spirit of holiness" (Rom. 1:4) that he is fully Lord: "God has made him both Lord and Christ, this Jesus whom you crucified" (Acts 2:36).

The risen Lord exists in a new way; resurrection is not resuscitation. The resurrection of Jesus is not like the raising up of Lazarus (see John 11:40–44). Jesus' physical appearance was changed even though he ate and drank with his disciples (Luke 24:42–43; Acts 10:41) and bore the mark of the nails and the lance (John 20:27). His disciples and friends did not recognize him at first   (e.g., Mary Magdalene, John 20:15–16; Cleopas and the other disciple, Luke 24:16; some doubted, Matt. 28:17). It is only through faith that the risen Lord is recognized.

As we look to the picture of Mary in the New Testament we see her relationship with Jesus developing as his lordship is progressively revealed. She is, as Vatican II taught, "inseparably linked with her Son's saving work (*Liturgy*, 103).

It is worth remarking that the great hymn of redemption in Philippians 2:5–11 finds echoes in the first chapter of Luke's Gospel. Jesus took the form of a slave (Greek, *doulos*; Phil. 2:7), Mary describes herself as a slave (Greek, *doulē*; Luke 1:38). Jesus humbled himself (Phil. 2:8), Mary describes her state as one of humiliation (Luke 1:48). God exalted Jesus (Phil. 2:9), the humble are exalted (Luke 1:52). Every knee shall bend . . . confess Jesus is Lord (Phil. 2:11), all generations will call Mary blessed (Luke 1:48). The similarity of Greek expressions throughout seems to suggest deliberate borrowing by Luke to illustrate the mystery of poverty being exalted in both Son and mother. God reigns in weakness, for in it his power is made perfect (see 2 Cor. 12:7–10, where this theme is developed).

Already in Bethlehem we see the mystery of a Son who does not wholly belong to his mother. She learns from the shepherds that he is "a Saviour who is Christ the Lord" (Luke 2:11, 17). Mary is shown as pondering this fact in her heart (Luke 2:19).

The next stage of revelation is the presentation in the temple. Here we have side by side two Jewish observances, the purification of the mother (see Lev. 12:6) and the ransoming of the firstborn (see Ex 13:2,12). Mary submits to the ritual of purification. This is part of a dominant lucan concern to show Joseph, Mary and Jesus very respectful of law, Jewish and civil (see Luke 2:4; 2:22–24 and later Jesus recognizes Caesar's rights, 20:25, and is declared innocent by the Roman authority, 23:22, 41). But the key to the incident as Luke narrates it—not without some confusion of the two Jewish customs—is the presentation in the temple. Here in two prophetic canticles Simeon proclaims that Mary's Son belongs to the world. He is:

> salvation . . . prepared in the presence of all the peoples,
> a light for revelation to the Gentiles, and for glory to
> [the] people Israel (Luke 2:30–32).

This is the oracle of the aged holy man who was waiting for the consolation of Israel (Luke 2:25; Greek, *paraklēsis*—the word echoes the comforter, *paraklētos*, of John 14:26).

The canticle of Simeon stresses that Jesus is for all peoples; its universalism evokes the prophecy of Zechariah:

> Sing and rejoice, O Daughter of Zion; for lo, I come and
> I will dwell in the midst of you, says the Lord. And
> many nations shall join themselves to the Lord on that
> day, and shall be my people; and I will dwell in the
> midst of you, and you shall know that the Lord of hosts
> has sent me to you (Zech. 2:10–11).

As Simeon blessed the parents of Jesus he foretells that

> this child is set for the fall and rise of many in Israel, and
> for a sign that is spoken against (and a sword will pass
> through your own soul also), that thoughts out of many
> hearts may be revealed (Luke 2:34–35).

This canticle introduces the notions of pain, of division—a suffering that Mary too will share. At the preaching of Jesus in future years the innermost thoughts of the scribes and pharisees will be revealed, and they, who were highly regarded, will be seen to fulfil the prophecy, "this people honors me with their lips, but their hearts are far from me" (Matt. 15:8; cf. Isa. 29:13).

Jesus will be rejected and Mary will share in the suffering. The old Simeon looks to the future with its messianic joy *and* its divisions. Jesus would later say that he came to bring not peace but a sword (Matt. 10:34–36).

Mary is to be tested in many ways, but she will survive the testing. As her Son begins to establish the true Israel, bonds of family will become less important than imperatives of faith. The first stage of Jesus' distancing himself from his family occurs when he is twelve years old. To the anxious question of Mary when she finds him in the temple after having been lost for three days, he replies, "Did you not know that I must be in my Father's house?". The will of the heavenly Father is even then of overmastering concern for Jesus. Many years later, when the family of Jesus looks for him, he gazes at his disciples and states that his true family are those who do the will of God (Mark 3:35). Mary will have to surrender her Son on Calvary and accept in faith John for her son (John 19:26–27). After all these trials she will emerge in the company of the one hundred twenty disciples as a true believer (Acts 1:14–15).

"Inseparably linked to her Son's saving work" (Vatican II: *Liturgy*,103) she continues to say to us as she said to the waiters at Cana, "do whatever he tells you" (John 2:5). These are her last recorded words in the gospels. This cooperation with her Son is developed more fully in the central document of the Second Vatican Council:

> She devoted herself totally as the handmaid of the Lord, to the person and work of her Son, under and with him, serving the mystery of redemption, by the grace of almighty God. Rightly, therefore, the Fathers see Mary not merely as passively engaged by God, but as freely cooperating in the work of humankind's salvation through faith and obedience (*Church*, 56).

This cooperation is understood in tradition in the

theology of the New Eve found as early as St. Justin (d. 165) and developed by St. Irenaeus (d.202). In its simplest form we can see it in the lapidary statement of St. Jerome: "Death through Eve, life through Mary" (*Letters*, 22, 21). This comparison of the two women is drawn out in great detail in the patristic period: Eve listened to the word of the serpent, Mary listened to the word of the angel. Eve heard evil news, Mary heard and accepted good news. Eve believed the serpent, Mary had faith in the angel. Eve was disobedient to God, Mary was obedient. Eve sinned by believing, Mary became holy through believing. Eve brought death and punishment, Mary brought life and hope. The guile of the serpent was overcome by the simplicity of the dove. By a virgin came death, by a virgin came life. Eve cooperated with the serpent to bring death, Mary cooperated with God to bring life. What was lost by one sex was restored by the same sex. It was through a man and a women that humankind was cast from paradise, it was through a man and a woman that humankind is linked to God. Eve is mother of the human race, Mary is mother of salvation. Glory was lost through Eve, it was restored through Mary. Childbirth for Eve was sorrow, for Mary it was joy. Paradise was lost through Eve, regained through Mary.

But even though the Fathers of the Church write extensively on the Eve-Mary parallel, they are more basically centered on the Adam-Christ analogy, which they found in St. Paul (Rom. 5:12ff). Mary's role is clearly a subordinate one, as is evident in all the early church writings. A passage from St, Justin reflects at once the flavor of the New Eve theology and the secondary role assigned to Mary:

[The Son] became man through a virgin, so that what began with the virgin's disobedience might be destroyed in the same manner. Eve, indeed, as an incorrupt virgin conceived the word that came from the serpent. Mary, however, received faith and joy when the angel Gabriel spoke to her, giving her the good news that the Spirit of God would come upon her and the power of the Most High would cover her, so that what would be born of her would be holy, the Son of God. She replied, "Be it done unto me according to thy word." There was born through her he by whom God destroys the serpent and angels and humans who become like the serpent. Those, however, who do penance for their wicked deeds and believe in him, he delivers from death (*Dialogue with Trypho*,100).

The intimate bond between Christ and Mary is again stressed by Pope Paul VI when he writes:

> In the Virgin Mary everything is relative to Christ and dependent on him....Genuine Christian piety has never failed to highlight the indissoluble link and essential relationship of the Virgin to the divine Savior (*Marialis Cultus*,25; cf. Vatican II: *Church*,66).

Jesus and Charismatic Renewal

As we turn to the charismatic renewal we note that at its heart is the affirmation, "Jesus is Lord." We have already seen that though the Holy Spirit is important in the spirituality of the charismatic renewal, nonetheless its core is not so much pneumatological (of the Spirit) as christological. The movement can look to Mary so that she may teach how Jesus is to be Lord. She is, as Paul VI reminds us, "a teacher of the spiritual life for individual Christians" (*Marialis Cultus*,21). The pope also quotes from the lovely fourth-century prayer of St. Ambrose:

> May the heart of Mary be in each Christian to proclaim the greatness of the Lord; may her spirit be in everyone to exult in God (*Expos. Ev. Luc.*,2,26).

Our assertion that Jesus is Lord will always be a practical program: we express what we would like to achieve in our hearts, our word and our deeds, but we know that we can always make more truthful what we proclaim with our lips. We have not come to that state in which "God may be everything to everyone"(1 Cor. 15:28). Meanwhile our life will revolve around the threefold "repent, believe and receive" the Holy Spirit.

We need to turn from sin, to allow ourselves to be purified and healed of what is not of God. Repentance is not a negative reality. We are led to it by God's kindness (see Rom. 2:4). It is his mercy that draws us to a change of life; it is not a matter of our own efforts, but a work of the Spirit through us bringing us to believe in the name of Jesus:

> There is salvation in no one else, for there is no other name under heaven given to us by which we must be saved (Acts 4:12).

Repentance is one facet of allowing Jesus to be Lord, and it is meant to be a joyful experience. It is in repentant love that we know two great attributes of God, his steadfast love and mercy (see Psalms,*passim*). For many persons it is only in the experience of need, in sinfulness, that they come to know a saving, a faithful, an ever-loving God.

We have already seen that "Jesus is Lord" was the first credal statement in the New Testament. Faith is a total "yes" to God. Its supreme model will always be the completeness of "let it be done to me according to your word" (Luke 1:38). It is, finally, as we repent and believe that we receive a further outpouring of the Holy Spirit which will enable us to confess Jesus to be Lord, for "No one can say 'Jesus is Lord' except by the Holy Spirit" (1 Cor. 12:3). We can then join in the universal chorus and with "every tongue confess that Jesus Christ is Lord to the glory of God the Father"(Phil. 2:11).

We have already seen that Mary was conformed to the pattern of this great hymn. Indeed, we find echoes of it elsewhere in the New Testament. At the last supper Jesus put aside his garments as he had put aside his glory (John 13:4; Phil. 2:7), he took up the form of a slave (John 13:5, Phil.2:7), he is rightly called Lord (John 13:13; Phil. 2:11). This was an example to the apostles to do likewise (John 13:15).

Inasmuch as Mary is the New Eve associated with the New Adam and she is the perfect model for our Christian lives, we must allow a new set of relationships to be established between us and Christ. We allow Jesus to be Lord to the extent that we are *with* him. There is a series of New Testament texts treating of our *being with* Jesus. It is something that is to be progressively realized in our lives. In baptism we are crucified with him (Rom. 6:6), buried with him (Rom. 6:4; Col. 2:12), so that we can be resurrected with him (Eph. 2:6; Col. 2:12). Our destiny is to be glorified with him (cf. Rom. 8:17). Just as we are dead with him (2 Tim. 2:11; Rom. 6:4,8) so we are to be living and reigning with him (2 Tim. 2:12)—that is, heirs with him (Rom. 8:17) and seated with him (Eph. 2:6).

This *being with* Christ in the Pauline writings is usually associated with *following* in the three synoptic gospels. Jesus summons the disciples to follow him (e.g., Mark 8:34). We must reckon the cost, for following means sacrifice (Luke 9:57–62; 5:11; 14:25–33), but this will bring the hundredfold reward (Matt. 19:29), not, however, without persecutions (Mark 10:28–30). Finally, to follow Jesus is be be with him (John 12:26).

Being with Christ and following him are spiritual states that involve growth. Allowing Jesus to be Lord in our lives is likewise gradual. Mary as our model said a total "yes" at the annunciation, but she was to learn the implications of this assent throughout her life. In charismatic renewal the perhaps exuberant early days of life in the Spirit gives way to a serious daily following of Christ. There will be need for continuous self-renewal—that is, we are to "put on the

Lord Jesus Christ, and make no provision for the flesh to gratify its desires" (Rom. 13:14). Mere confession of the lordship of Jesus with our lips is not without continuous conversion: "Not everyone who says to me 'lord, lord' shall enter the kingdom of heaven, but the one who does the will of my Father who is in heaven." (Matt. 7:21).

The New Eve, obedient to the word of God, is the pattern of our submission to God. What is involved is a continued seeking of the will of God. In the charismatic renewal we are accustomed to being led to know God's will through his word. Indeed, the most common of all charisms found in the renewal is a new ability to read the Scriptures, so that they come alive. This gift recalls the experience of the two disciples on the road to Emmaus who said, "Did not our hearts burn within us while he talked to us on the road, while he opened to us the Scriptures?" (Luke 24:32).

Daily reading of the scriptures is very common in charismatic renewal. Besides this private reading of the word of God, it is shared at prayer meetings. The gift of prophecy also manifests to us the will of God. But in the reading of Scripture and in the verification of prophecy there is need for wisdom and at times the charism of discernment. What is important here is to learn what is the will of God so that we can be filled with it "to lead a life worthy of the Lord, fully pleasing to him, bearing fruit in every good work and increasing in the knowledge of God" (Col. 1:10).

Another way of coming to knowledge of the will of God is the wise advice of others. Through our brothers and sisters we learn more accurately what is mere human wisdom and thus folly in the eyes of God (see 1 Cor. 1:18–25). Being gathered in the name of the Lord, he will be present to us in the Spirit (see Matt. 18:20) and thus we can be more assured of finding the right path. Obedience is a primary demand of the lordship of Jesus: "if you know these things, blessed are you if you do them" (John 13:17). If we love Christ we will keep his word (John 14:23); more than that, we are his friends if we do what he commands us (see John 15:14).

Mary, the New Eve, was obedient. She also undid the work of the serpent. In the charismatic renewal there is serious account taken of " that ancient serpent, who is called the Devil and Satan, the deceivers of the whole world" (Rev. 12:9). An important aspect of the lordship of Jesus is his victory over the powers of evil. Jesus came to destroy the works of the Devil (see 1 John 3:8). The passion was a time of intense activity on the part of Satan (see Luke 4:13; 22:53; John 12:2, 27), but the ruler of the world has no power over Jesus (see John 14:30). Satan once dared to offer Jesus the kingdoms of the world (Luke 4:6), but now he knows that the world belongs to the crucified and glorified Christ (see Matt. 28:18; Phil. 2:9–11).

Though the radical defeat of Satan is guaranteed, we must accept in our lives the implications of this victory. The enemy will continue to attack us, especially by temptation (see 1 Thess. 3:5). Prowling like a greedy lion, he seeks victims to devour (1 Pet. 5:8). Satan, who loves to disguise himself as an angel of light (see 2 Cor. 11:14), is a formidable adversary (2 Cor. 2:11), but we must not be afraid of him. On the contrary, clothed with spiritual armor (Eph. 6:10–18), we are to stand firm and resist him (see James 4:7; 1 Pet. 5:8–9), knowing that "no one begotten of God commits sin; rather, God protects the one begotten by him, and so the evil one cannot touch him" (1 John 5:19). In the end, Satan will be utterly crushed (see Rev. 12:10– 12; 20:10).

Charismatic renewal must keep a balance here between two quite opposite errors. One mistake is to neglect to take account of the powerful adversary. Pope Paul VI noted in November 1972:

> The question of the Devil and the influence he can exert on individual persons, as well as on communities, whole societies or events, is a very important chapter of Catholic doctrine that is given little attention today. It should be studied again.

The other error is to concentrate overmuch on the Devil

or to become fearful of his activity. The mature Christian view is to take cognizance of the real power of evil, and look to the name of Jesus for protection and deliverance. Mary is seen as conquerer of evil more by obedience to God than by direct confrontation. This is a consistant feature of the New Eve theology. Furthermore, in the liturgy of the East and West, the emphasis is on the seed of the woman who will crush the serpent's head (Gen. 3:15). A characteristic text from the Matins of the annunciation in the Byzantine rite reads:

> Today all creation rejoices, for the archangel says to thee, "Hail! Blessed art thou, O pure and holy, undefiled and spotless." Today the proud insolence of the serpent is brought low, for the fetters of the curse laid on our forefather are loosened.

More explicit is St. Ephrem (d. 373) who prays to Mary to protect him lest Satan rejoice over him (*Orat. ad B.V.M.*).

We can point to the lordship of Christ in two feasts in the Western church, the ascension and Christ the King. The first is the mystery by which he was established as Lord according to the primitive catechetical formula recorded by Paul,

> Great indeed, we confess, is the mystery of our religion:
> he was manifested in the flesh, vindicated in the Spirit,
> seen by angels, preached among the nations, believed
> on in the world, taken up into glory (1 Tim. 3:16).

The second feast was established by Pope Pius XI. It can focus our thoughts on how we are to cooperate in the universal kingship of Christ. He was reluctant to accept the title, though it had been foretold that he would be a king (Luke 1:32–33). His reticence in this matter was clearly to avoid confirming distorted messianic expectations. Thus after the bread miracle the people wished to make him king. His response was to withdraw to the hills by himself (John 6:15). When he does accept the title it is only to emphasize the second coming (see John 1:49, 51; Matt. 25:31–35), or the otherworldly nature of the kingdom (see John 18:33–37). The kingdom is essentially future, but already it is making its appearance in our midst (see Luke 11:20), for "he has delivered us from the dominion of darkness and transferred us to the kingdom of his beloved Son in whom we have redemption, the forgiveness of sins" (Col. 1:13–14).

Through baptism we are sharers in the kingship of Christ. We are to implant the marks of the kingdom in society, to work for the establishment of

> an eternal and universal kingdom, a kingdom of truth and life, a kingdom of holiness and grace, a kingdom of justice, love and peace (Preface of the feast of Christ the King).

Charismatic renewal will have its own particular accent in working for the kingdom of God. This will involve deep renewal which is person and communitarian, as well as "the self-abnegation of a holy life" (Vatican II:*Church*,36). A heightened awareness of charism will be an important dimension in living out the teaching, "all things are yours, you are Christ's, and Christ is God's" (1 Cor. 3:23).

The call of the Second Vatican Council to the laity in particular is that

> by their secular activity they must aid one another to greater holiness of life so that the world may be filled with the Spirit of Christ and may the more effectively attain its destiny in justice, in love and in peace (*Church*,36).

This challenge calls for a response that is authentically marian. It demands from us Mary's answer, "let it be done to me according to thy word" (Luke 1:38), a saying strikingly similar to "thy will be done" of the Our Father (Matt. 6:10). But it will not always be immediately clear what is true and life-giving, what is holy and grace-filled, what is just, loving and peaceful. God asks from us an antecedent acceptance of his will, just as he did from Mary. She said "yes" and waited for God's will to be made manifest in the years that followed.

Once again we return to the crucial idea of receptivity. Mary said her *fiat*: she was the receptive virgin, open to receive God's grace, open to hear and do his will. Paradoxically, the more Jesus appeared to withdraw from his mother, the more he became Lord for her. He is fully Lord for her and for the church as he departs in the ascension, leaving her in the care of the Beloved Disciple. This is a culmination of Mary's "yes" to the ways of God.

Chapter IV

Mary, Woman of Faith

WE HAVE SEEN that from very early times the church developed the typology of Mary as the New Eve. The comparison of the first woman and the Blessed Virgin stresses Mary's faith: she believed the angel, whereas Eve believed the serpent. Mary's faith is so central to her spirituality and to ours that it merits an extended treatment.

Until recent decades Catholic catechetics stressed almost exclusively the intellectual aspect of faith: in the face of Protestant and later fideist downplaying of the intellect in the act of faith, Catholic theology emphasized faith as an assent to God's revealed truth. It indicated the response of the Christian when confronted with truths revealed by God. This is correct, but is only a *partial* account of faith.

The period since the Second Vatican Council has witnessed a greater stress on *biblical* faith, which is more the response of the total person to God. It is a full "yes," an *amen*—"so be it"— to the word, the promises, the commands of God. It involves trust, fidelity, obedience, as well as the acceptance of truths. We find it exemplified above all in Mary whom we describe simply as "woman of faith."

The central incident in the New Testament for an appreciation of Mary's faith is clearly the annunciation. We might begin a study of this incident by recalling the Preface of the feast in the Roman rite. It gives a reflection on the meaning of the event in terms of salvation history:

He came to save humankind by becoming a man himself. The Virgin Mary, receiving the angel's message in faith, conceived by the power of the Spirit and bore your Son in purest love. In Christ, the eternal truth, your promise to Israel came true. In Christ, the hope of all peoples, humankind's hope, was realized beyond all expectation.

The event as recorded by St. Luke is narrated in the highly stylized literary form used in the Bible for the solemn announcement of a birth or of a mission of singular importance—for example, the birth of Isaac (Gen. 17), the call of Moses (Exod. 3) and of Gideon (Judg. 6), the birth of Samson (Judg. 13) and of John the Baptist (Luke 1). In them we find a heavenly messenger, the reaction of fear, a name given, future accomplishments stated, and a sign foretold.

Luke uses this traditional structure in the account of the annunciation to Mary. But at the same time, he, in addition, highlights contrasts with the annunciation to Zechariah. A key to the comparison of these two New Testament annunciations is, of course, the belief of Mary compared with the unbelief of Zechariah.

At the time of the annunciation Mary is engaged, but not formally married, to Joseph. The angel's greeting is not the customary one, "Peace," but a messianic call: *"chaire, rejoice."* The Greek word is found in various places in the Old Testament translation where there is a context of messianic joy—for example, Zephaniah 3:14 (a passage that Luke echoes several times in the story of the annunciation). She is addressed as "O favored one" and is told that the Lord is with her.

The phrase "the Lord is with you" occurs very frequently in the Scriptures. It indicates God's support, protection, care for a person. The angel's message shows *how* Mary has found favor with God: she is to bear a son, he will be called Jesus, he will be great and kingly and his reign will be eternal. The significance of Mary's question, "how shall this be ...," is by no means clear. At the very least it shows us that as Mary could be deeply troubled and afraid (see Luke 1:29–30), she could also fail to understand.

She is then given a sign: her aged cousin has conceived a child. She is told, moreover, that nothing is impossible with God (1:37). This final statement gives a basis for faith. It states a conviction that is recorded several times in the Bible—always in the context of a serious difficulty or human impossibility. It is said to Abraham when God's promise of posterity through the elderly and barren Sarah seems incredible (Gen. 18:14). It is said to the inhabitants of Jerusalem when the army of the Chaldeans has begun a siege: the Lord could protect them (Jer. 32:27). Job speaks thus when he recognizes anew the power of God (Job 42:2). In the synoptic tradition we learn that the salvation of the rich is indeed difficult, but not impossible to God (see Matt. 19:26).

Mary's response is to proclaim herself a slave of the Lord. Her position is one of total obedience. We have already noted that her reply—usually translated "let it be done to me according to your word" (Luke 1:38)—suggests in Greek a joyful and enthusiastic response to the word. Again, for the Hebrews the "word" is always open to mean an action as well as what is said. Mary is thus declaring herself completely submissive to God's plan—his word and action. It is a total "yes" of all her being. Moreover, she acquiesces on the basis of rather limited information. Given the messianic expectations of her people, which were overmaterialistic and nationalistic, there is little in the angel's message to correct these views. The great texts on the suffering servant (e.g. Isa. 53; Zech. 12:10) were not widely seen as messianic in Mary's time. Her compliance with the will of God is total and unconditional, based on the strength of the fact that nothing is impossible to God (1:37).

The Second Vatican Council speaks of Mary's beginning now a pilgrimage of faith (*Church*,58). A pilgrimage is a journey to a holy place. Mary begins a pilgrimage that will take her to Calvary, the holy place of sacrifice, and to the upper room sanctified by the last supper where she will again receive an outpouring of the Holy Spirit.

We can understand Mary's faith more profoundly if we contrast her with Abraham "our father in faith" (first eucharistic prayer of the Roman rite). This comparison is at least implicit in Luke. We have already seen that the expression "with God nothing is impossible" was both addressed to Abraham and Mary (Gen. 18:14; Luke 1:37). Luke recalls the promise made to Abraham (Luke 1:55; Gen. 13:15f; 22:17f). Mary and Abraham are both praised for their faith (Luke 1:45; Gen. 15:6). Both were asked to sacrifice their sons; each ascended a hill of sacrifice. But whereas Abraham was spared the actual death of his son (Gen. 22:12), Mary was to see her Son die (John 19:25-30). Again, Abraham "obeyed when he was called to go to a place that he was to receive as an inheritance," and his descendants were to be as numerous as the stars of heaven (Gen. 15:5-6); Mary's obedience led her to Calvary where, in the person of the Beloved Disciple, she was to receive all humankind as her offspring (John 19:25-27). In Mary and in Abraham faith and obedience merge in a total "yes" to God.

The unity of faith and obedience in Mary emerges in another way elsewhere in Luke. The evangelist recalls the incident of the woman in the crowd who cries out in praise of Mary: "Blessed is the womb that bore you, and the breasts that you sucked" (Luke 11:27). Jesus immediately points to where the true blessedness of Mary lies: "Blessed rather are those who hear the word of God and keep it" (Luke 11:28). More important, then, than physical relationship to Jesus is obedient faith.

The same transition occurs in the visitation scene. Elizabeth praises Mary as mother of the Messiah, "Blessed are you among women and blessed is the fruit of your womb" (Luke 1:42). But she goes on to show where Mary's true blessedness lies: "Blessed is she who believed that there would be a fulfilment of what was spoken to her from the Lord" (Luke 1:45). It is as a woman of faith that Mary is blessed.

The Second Vatican Council states that Mary "consenting to the word of God, became the Mother of Jesus" and that through faith and obedience she cooperated in the work of man's salvation (*Church*,56). The same idea is repeated later by the council: "through faith and obedience she gave birth to the very Son of the Father" (*Church*,63).

The Role of Faith in Charismatic Renewal

Faith is at the heart of the endeavors of the charismatic renewal. At its heart is the conviction that God still speaks to and guides his church. Like Mary at the annunciation we have to be alert to the ways in which God's angel, his message, may come. God can speak to us in the prayer-meeting environment, in personal prayer, in the events of our lives. We are to know him as Emmanuel, God-with-us. His presence may be mainly consolation, or threat, or rebuke, or a call to conversion. The appropriate response will be faith, acceptance of whatever God wills, because he wants it and because he loves us.

It is indeed through faith that we accept the basic truth that God loves us a way that is individual and personal. This truth becomes salvific when a person affirms it by word, action and lifestyle. The statement "God loves me" is, as we have noted already, the foundation of the spirituality of the charismatic renewal. It is this that allows us to trust God, to be fully open to his will for us. Until that truth is soundly grasped, fear will keep us from advancing toward God. Our "yes" must be unconditional, like Mary's, to a future known only to God.

Faith always has its dark, as well as its light, side. Often indeed we walk in a half-light. Mary knew the darkness of faith and so do we. But what was significant for her is not so much the darkness of faith in which she lived, but rather the light she received. She walked in the light of faith, a light that only partially illumined the darkness for her. She did not know where her "yes" would lead her, but she travelled by what light she received to Calvary and the Upper Room. We too must look to the light we receive about God and his love for us and be prepared to walk in that light. In other words, the significant factor we share with Mary is not that we both know darkness, but rather that we must walk in whatever glimmer of light God wills to bestow on us.

Affirming with our minds and hearts the fundamental truth of God's love, we can then accept the second great religious truth—namely, that God wills to save. We learn that apart from Jesus "there is salvation in no one else, for there is no other name under heaven given among men by which we must be saved" (Acts 4:12).

Acceptance of the truth that God saves can be no mere intellectual act: it demands an obedient faith, a marian disposition of "let it be done to me according to your word" (Luke 1:38). We need salvation and this, as Paul proclaims, is through faith:

> For I am not ashamed of the gospel: it is the power of God for salvation to every one who has faith, to the Jew first and also to the Greek. For in it the righteousness of God is revealed through faith for faith; as it is written, "the person who through faith is righteous shall live" (Rom. 1:16–17).

This dense statement enunciates first that the gospel manifests God's righteousness—that is, his saving justice, his basic attitude, which is that of reconciling us to himself in Christ. The meaning of the phrase "through faith for faith" is not fully clear. It could mean "from initial to more perfect faith" or else that out faith brings us to what God plans for us. Paul then cites the prophet Habakkuk promising life at the time of the Chaldean invasion. For us the life that faith brings is salvation.

The faith that leads to salvation is a divine gift, just as was Mary's faith: "Mary had a faith that your Spirit prepared and a love that never knew sin, for you kept her sinless from the first moment of her conception" (prayer from the feast of the immaculate conception, Roman rite). The church prays for a reflection of that faith: "Trace in our actions the lines of her love and in our hearts her readiness of faith" (ibid.).

Faith is a gift that leads to still more profound gifts. It is something that touches us deeply, in the depths of our being (the "heart", in Scripture), and then must be shared with others. The progression is outlined by Paul:

> The word is near you, on your lips and in your heart (that is, the word of faith that we preach); because, if you confess with your lips that Jesus is Lord and believe in your heart that God raised him from the dead, you will be saved (Rom. 10:8–10).

Here we have something of the complexity of faith. It is primarily a matter of the heart, of our inner selves. To this personal appropriation corresponds the confession that Jesus is Lord. His lordship must be proclaimed in word and deed. There will thus be conformity between what is in our heart and what we profess. This leads to the fullness of life that is salvation.

Mary, as we noted in an earlier chapter, can truly be said to have been saved: she is "the most excellent fruit of the redemption" (Vatican II:*Liturgy*, 103). Salvation for us is a gradual process, a faith-orientated and faith-directed life. For Mary it lies primarily in the two gifts of the immaculate conception and lifelong sinlessness. But though saved from the first moment of her existence she nevertheless had to walk the path of faith and she learned ever more profoundly that her Son is Lord.

What we have been saying about faith and salvation has already brought us to the third stage of the basic charismatic spirituality—namely, new life. After recognizing and trusting God's love, accepting Jesus as Savior, we are then called to open ourselves to new life. But this, we have seen in St. Paul's teaching, is "from faith and through faith," whichever interpretation we may take of Romans 1:17. Charismatic renewal goes beyond these three stages, which culminate in a profound personal conversion, for it stresses charisms, the gift of the Spirit. We shall study the charisms in detail later. Our concern for the moment is to see that they rely on faith for their acceptance and exercise.

Charisms and Faith

The charisms that we encounter in the charismatic renewal and elsewhere in the church are sometimes natural gifts that are intensified by God's further gifts or are given a new direction so that the area of their exercise becomes more explicitly the kingdom. At other times they are gifts that are beyond natural ability.

Under the first heading we have gifts such as teaching, administration and tongues. These are natural abilities. One can have a natural talent and so be a good teacher. This can be further improved by training and practice. But the charism of teaching can be added by God so that one has a new ability for communication in the service of the kingdom. Indeed all communication of divine truth probably demands a charism or a passing influence of the Spirit if the word is to take root in the heart of the hearer. The second example, administration, is again a natural gift that can be improved by the learning of further skills. But the wise and prudent administration of persons and things in the service of the kingdom may call for further gifts or charisms of the Spirit.

In the case of these two examples, and of many similar gifts mentioned in the New Testament, such as service, exhortation, and works of mercy (see Rom. 12:7-8), faith is important: it enables us to recognize God at work in the gift. It can also lead us to pray for further increase of the gift.

The gift of tongues, too, is a natural ability—almost anybody can babble. What brings it into the sphere of religious experience is that the sounds occur in the context of prayer and there is an act of faith in the fact that these meaningless sounds can be used by the Spirit within us to utter the prayer that we cannot articulate (see Rom. 8:26–28). Clearly, faith can help the gift of tongues to grow; it will give confidence in the exercise of the gift; it will make the individual more aware of the indwelling Spirit.

Other gifts go beyond natural ability. Examples of these would be prophecy and healing. The gift of prophecy may be latent and not recognized as such. Through baptism we share in the prophetic office of Christ (see Vatican II:*Church*,35). In daily life, in the family, in work situations, in religious community, we can get ideas without recognizing that they may be from God. It is through faith that we recognize the prophetic gift that takes the form of speaking out and acting on God's behalf. Faith enables us to recognize that an inner word may be from God.

The charism of prophecy as commonly experienced in the charismatic renewal involves both the explicit recognition that an inner word may be coming from God as well as the grace needed to speak out this word, There can, of course, be no certainty on the part of the prophet that the word spoken out is truly from God. Religious experiences need verification apart from the experience: Mary was given a sign to confirm the angel's word (Luke 1:36). In the case of prophecy, confirmation comes from the discernment of others, especially of those who have the gift of prophecy themselves (see 1 Cor. 14:29).

The gift of healing, or more properly "gifts of healings" (1 Cor. 12:9, in the Greek text), clearly demands faith for its exercise. The one who prays for healing must have faith in the Lord who heals. Healing does not necessarily depend on the faith of the sick person, though this is helpful and can be required. Faith was normally demanded even in the ministry of Jesus. He said to the Canaanite woman, "O woman, great is your faith! Be it done for you as you desire" (Matt. 15:28). To the centurian he exclaimed, "Truly, I

say to you, not even in Israel have I found such faith...
Go, be it done for you as you have believed" (Matt. 8:10,
13). When he saw the faith of those who let the paralytic
down through the roof, he healed him (Matt. 9:2). He
could not, however, work any mighty deeds in Nazareth,
because of their unbelief (Matt. 13:58).

Healing has two aspects: it is an act of divine compassion for the sick person and it is a sign of the eventual
triumph over all evils including sickness and death. Our
victories over illness are temporary—Lazarus died again.
We await the blessed hope of full victory. Mary is "the sign
of hope for the pilgrim church" (Preface of the assumption,
Roman rite): she is fully glorified. Where she already is, we
are to come. She is at the term of her pilgrimage of faith.
We can rely on God to give us whatever healing—spiritual,
emotional, physical—we need to reach her glorified state.

There is, then, in the charisms an element of faith: they
grow through faith and faith allows us to detect God at
work through them. Faith is further required that the
charisms redound to the praise of God. Thus, we read in
the First Letter of Peter:

> As each one has received a gift, employ it for one
> another, as good stewards of Cod's varied grace:
> whoever speaks, as one who utters oracles of God;
> whoever renders service, as one who renders it by the
> strength God supplies; in order that in everything God
> may be glorified through Jesus Christ (4:10-11).

Faith is the response to God who has revealed himself in
word and deed as the faithful God, who loves steadfastly,
who continues to show mercy. Just as God calls us and
sends us, he also equips us so that we "are not lacking in
any spiritual gift" (1 Cor. 1:7). The Second Letter of Peter
gives us a wide vision of God's action in us. It goes from a
proclamation of God's work in us to the heart of the
mystery of divine adoption:

His divine power has granted to us all things that per-
tain to life and godliness, through the knowledge of him
who called us to his own glory and excellence, by which
he has granted to us his precious and very great promises, that through these you may escape from the corruption that is in the world because of passion, and
become partakers of the divine nature (1:3-4).

Sharing in the divine nature is a gradual process. It will,
indeed, be an eternal growth. Mary already shared in it
through the gift of grace given in the immaculate conception. Throughout her life it developed. In the vision of
God her assumed state will partake of it ever more fully.
Our partial sharing now of the divine adoption is an entering
into what Mary already enjoys more completely.

The communion of saints is a central mystery of our
faith. It underlines both the sharing of holy things and the
family life of holy persons who are one in God. Through
faith there is a vision or knowledge of deeper dimensions in
our lives.

Faith is not, however, direct knowledge of God. It is
mediated through the church, and especially through apostolic witnesses. In the First Letter of John we read:

that which we have seen and heard we proclaim to you,
that you may have fellowship [koinonia] with us; and
our fellowship [koinonia] is with the Father and with his
Son, Jesus Christ (1:3).

That is to say, we enter into a relationship with the
apostles; they in turn are related to the Father in and
through his Son. Our knowledge of Christ is from the
Scriptures; it is not given to the individual directly. When
we profess the church to be apostolic we are in part saying
that we have communion (koinonia) with the apostles
through the word they preached. We still continue to make
an act of faith in what the apostles preached and the early
church believed.

When we look at the upper room after the ascension we note three groups of witnesses to Jesus (Acts 1:13–14). First there are the Eleven who shared the public life of Jesus "from the baptism of John until the day he was taken up" (Acts 1:22) and who were witnesses of the resurrection. The second group is that of the women, witnesses to the empty tomb (Luke 23:55; 24:3, 22–23). And there was "Mary and his brothers," witnesses to the infancy and hidden life. We receive our faith in the birth and early life of Jesus through Mary and his family. They are a source of tradition about Jesus.

It follows that the more we have the mind of Mary as we contemplate the life of Jesus, the closer we draw to him. She has a mother's understanding of Jesus, an accurate and balanced understanding. This was given to her for herself and for the church. How she grew in faith and in the knowledge of her Son belongs to a study of Mary and the Word.

Chapter V

Mary and the Word of God

A THEME strikingly emphasized by Luke is that of Mary's failing to understand (1:34; 2:19, 50). She is the woman of faith, knowing its darkness as well as its light. Inasmuch as the most difficult of these texts is the third, we shall begin with it. It occurs in the story of the finding in the temple (Luke 2:41–51), a narrative that can be read at diverse levels. Investigation into it reveals more profoundly the woman of faith who pondered the word of God. The text is a familiar one:

> Now his parents went to Jerusalem every year at the feast of the Passover. And when he was twelve years old they went up according to custom; and when the feast was ended, as they were returning, the boy Jesus stayed behind in Jerusalem. His parents did not know it but, supposing him to be in the company, they went a day's journey, and they sought him among their kinsfolk and acquaintances; and when they did not find him, they returned to Jerusalem seeking him. After three days they found him in the temple, sitting among the teachers, listening to them and asking them questions; and all who heard him were amazed at his understanding and his answers. And when they saw him they were astonished; and his mother said to him, "Son, why have you treated us so? Behold your father and I have been looking for you anxiously." And he said to them, "How is it that

you sought me? Did you not know that I must be in my
Father's house?" And they did not understand the saying
which he spoke to them. And he went down with them
and came to Nazareth, and was obedient to them; and
his mother kept all these things in her heart.

At a certain level, the story is one of misunderstandings.
Mary and Joseph are under the misapprehension that Jesus
is in the company of relatives and acquaintances returning
home from the feast. It is only after a day's journey that
they realize he is missing. They return to Jerusalem and,
after a day or more of anxious searching, they find him in
the temple. The boy Jesus seems to accuse them of further
misunderstanding: "Did you not know that I must be in
my Father's house?" They do not understand his words.

There is an unusual shift from the Nazareth use of the title
"father"—applied to Joseph (2:48)—to a different use in
the phrase "my Father's house" (2:49).

The statement "they did not understand" can refer to the
whole incident or to the abrupt introduction of the heavenly
Father, or to both.

There are several points to be noted in the narrative. We
cannot determine whether Jesus was in a teaching or learning
role: Jesus sat to teach (e.g., Matt. 5:1; Luke 5:3); Paul was
trained at the feet of Gamaliel (Acts 22:3).

Then there is the theme of surprise and amazement. The
term applied to "all who heard him" (2:47) is very strong:
the wisdom of his answers is a cause of *utter surprise*.
Again there is a strong term used about Mary and Joseph:
"when they saw him they were *astonished* (2:48). Mary
then says that they were deeply worried (2:48). Jesus' reply
indicates surprise: "How is it that you sought me?" The
question is addressed to both of them and it is a reply to
their astonishment and anxiety. There is, moreover, a
sharp contrast between the surprising understanding of
Jesus and the lack of understanding on the part of Mary
and Joseph. What they do not understand is a *word*, which
may indicate a saying or an event.

We might ask why this incident is singled out from the whole hidden life of Jesus that stretches from the presentation in the temple to his baptism. One reason is that the evangelist wishes to draw our attention to a deeper meaning in terms of the Old Testament. Lying behind the story is Malachi 3:1–3:

> The Lord whom you seek will suddenly come to his temple ... the messenger of the covenant ... behold he is coming ... he will sit as a refiner and purifier of silver, and he will purify the sons of Levi....

At the age of twelve Jesus is being portrayed as the Lord of the temple. Already he is beginning to fulfil messianic prophecies.

Another reason may be that this incident could be the first time that Jesus appeared to distance himself from his family ties: his heavenly Father and his house make demands superior to the relationship he had to Joseph and Mary. That would be sufficient grounds for its retention in the early tradition and its incorporation into the infancy gospel.

But in the total context of the gospel there is yet another level of meaning. An examination of the incident discloses several motifs, each of which emerges in full clarity only in the passion and resurrection narratives. The full richness of the incident is found only if we take it to be a prophetic incident.

The Old Testament prophets were accustomed to perform actions that were symbolic, pointed to a future reality, or were seen to have a deeper significance. Thus Ezekiel cooked food (Ezek. 4:9–15), cut his hair (5:1–15), dressed as an exile (12:1–20). Jeremiah broke an earthen pot (Jer. 19:1–15). Amos saw a plummet (Amos 7:7-9). Zechariah took two shepherd's staffs (Zech. 11:4–17).

The narration of the finding in the temple is of this genre. It is at one level a simple incident from the boyhood of Jesus; at another it is a prophetic foreshadowing of his death and resurrection.

There are eight themes in the narrative that will be found again in the last pages of Luke's Gospel. The incident takes place in *Jerusalem* (2:41, 43, 45), where the account of Jesus' death and resurrection is also central. Indeed, the whole Gospel of Luke is written as a journey up to Jerusalem (9:51, 53; 13:22; 17:11). Jesus is found in the *temple* (2:46); the temple figures in the passion narrative, for Jesus was charged with speaking against it, and Luke's Gospel ends where it began—in the temple (1:8; 24:53). It is *passover* time (2:41, 42); Jesus dies at passover time (22:1). There is a loss for *three days* (2:46); Jesus' own predictions of his passion stressed three days (9:22), and the resurrection is on the third day (21:46; 24:7). There is the theme of *accomplishment/fulfillment* (2:43); the Scriptures must be fulfilled (24:44). Jesus *must* (in the Greek, *dei*) be in his Father's house; in the passion and resurrection accounts there is a great emphasis on the need for the Scriptures to be fulfilled and for the Father's will to be accomplished (with the same word, *dei*—22:37; 24:7, 26, 44). Mary and Joseph do *not understand* (2:50); incomprehension is a characteristic of the resurrection passages (24:11, 25, 41, 45). Jesus is sought after his burial (24:5, 23–24).

We are alerted to the existence of deeper meanings in Luke's writings when he observes that "they did not understand....his mother kept all these things in her heart" (2:50–51). It is clear that the discovery of the more profound meaning of Scripture is the fruit of continued meditation. It is not explicitly stated—nor is it excluded—that the discovery of the fuller meaning of this incident was the fruit of Mary's meditation. At the very least we have here the result of the early church's reflection on the childhood of Jesus.

There is no need to be embarrassed by the lack of understanding on the part of Joseph and Mary. It was genuine and need not be explained away: they did not understand his reply, they did not understand the meaning of the whole incident. Luke wants us to look on Mary pondering in her heart during the years in Nazareth. He had earlier shown Mary reflecting in her heart in the second passage to which we now turn.

The shepherds heard the angels' message, they went to Bethlehem and told what they had heard. Luke gives three reactions:

> *All who heard* it wondered at what the shepherds told them. But *Mary* kept all these things, pondering them in her heart. And the *shepherds* returned, glorifying and praising God for all they had heard and seen (2:18-20).

It is a strong Greek expression that is translated "kept all these things": it suggests that she retained them with the greatest care. She kept these things—literally, "all these words"—and pondered them. For this last, Luke uses a compound Greek verb that means "throw side by side" (*sym-ballein*). There were so many things she needed to meditate upon: the birth in Bethlehem, the providential nature of the census bringing them to the royal city so that the prophecy of Micah (ch. 4-5) might be fulfilled, her role, her Son's future (Lk 1:32-33). She reflects on all these things to bring out their inner meaning. In this she resembles the wise man in Sirach:

> He who devotes himself to the study of the law of the Most High will seek out the wisdom of all the ancients, and will be concerned with the prophecies; he will preserve the discourse of notable men and penetrate the subtleties of parables; he will seek out the hidden meaning of proverbs and be at home with the obscurities of parables (Sir. 39:1-3).

Mary is entitled to the praise of the same author:

> Blessed is he who concerns himself with these things, and he who lays them to heart will become wise. For if he does them, he will be strong for all things, for the light of the Lord is his path (Sir. 50:28-29).

We can interpret the Bethlehem scene in terms of what has been called the foundational parable—namely, that of the sower (Luke 8:4–15). The mysterious group, called by Luke "all who heard it" and who wondered, might be compared to the seed that fell along the path (8:12): there is no record of their coming to salvation and faith. The shepherds who glorified and praised God (2:20) resemble the seed that fell on the rock, those who "when they hear the word receive it with joy, but have no root, they believe for a while and in time of temptation fall away" (8:13). The shepherds were to have no significance so far as we know: the word did not take root in them. But Mary resembles the seed falling on good soil, "those who, hearing the word, hold it fast with an honest and good heart, and bring forth fruit with patience" (8:15).

The third text related to Mary's lack of understanding is the question to the angel, "how can this be?" (Luke 1:34). The meaning and implications of this question are not clear to scholars. At the very least, however, we can say that Mary, the perfect woman of faith, could find God's ways difficult to understand.

The angel states in reply to her that the Holy Spirit will come upon her. On hearing this Mary says her *fiat* to God's plans for her. In the Byzantine rite there is a charming dialogue between Mary and the angel, reflecting the New Eve theology. It is found in the Great Vespers of the feast of the annunciation:

> Revealing to thee the preeternal counsel, Gabriel came and stood before thee, O maid; and greeting thee, he said: "Hail, thou earth that has not been sown; hail, thou burning bush that remains unconsumed; hail, thou unsearchable depth; hail, thou bridge that leads to heaven, and ladder raised on high that Jacob saw; hail, thou divine jar of manna; hail, thou deliverance from the curse; hail, thou restoration of Adam, the Lord is with thee" (cf. Exod. 3:2; 16:33; Gen. 28:12).
>
> "Thou dost appear to me in the form of a man," said

the undefiled maid to the chief of the heavenly hosts: "how then dost thou speak to me of things that pass man's power? For thou hast said that God shall be with me, and shall take up his dwelling in my womb; how, tell me, shall I become the spacious habitation and the holy place of him that rides upon the cherubim (cf. Ps. 17:11)? Do not beguile me with deceit: for I have not known pleasure, I have not entered into wedlock. How then shall I bear a child?"

"When God so wishes," said the bodiless angel, "the order of nature is overcome, and what is beyond man comes to pass. Believe that my sayings are true, O all-holy lady, utterly without spot." And she cried aloud, "Let it be done unto me according to thy word: and I shall bear him that is without flesh, who shall borrow flesh from me, that through this mingling he may lead man up to his ancient glory, for he alone has power so to do."

These three texts (Luke 1:34; 2:19; 2:51), each in its own way, invite us to consider further aspects of the parable of the sower, especially the seed on good soil. It is in patience that the seed bears fruit, but first it must be sown in a heart that is "honest and good" (Luke 8:15). In Mary, the receptive virgin, the word of God is held fast, and in time yields its hundredfold (Luke 8:8).

Charisms, Scripture and Renewal

We have already noted the important role of Scripture in the charismatic renewal and we have emphasized that the desire to read the Bible is frequently joined to a charism or new ability to understand it. The centrality of Scripture is not confined to the prayer meeting, though it is very biblical both in the readings and in the hymns, which are scriptural for the most part. All Scripture, but most notably in liturgical celebrations, takes on a new freshness and urgency.

Charismatic renewal can look to Mary as its model as she pondered the word of God in her heart. Her reflection was lifelong. Before the annunciation she shared the age-old expectation of her people. After the annunciation she had still more reason to search the Scriptures to learn about her Son and about her role. We can only imagine her eagerness each Sabbath to hear the law and the prophets read. Our approach to Scripture, especially as proclaimed in liturgical worship, needs to reflect Mary's Sabbath dispositions.

This can be viewed another way by looking at the parable of the sower once more. We can be thankful to God that through "the immeasurable riches of his grace" (Eph. 2:7) we are seed on good soil. God's grace in us has not been in vain (see 1 Cor. 15:10). The basic orientation of our lives is that of hearing the word, holding it fast in an open and honest heart and bearing fruit through perseverance (Luke 8:15). But the word of God is continually being sown in our midst. Last Sunday we heard the word of God in a liturgical assembly. What fruit has it borne? Has the Devil taken it from our hearts? Has temptation diverted our attention? Have the cares and riches of this life prevented its maturing (see Luke 8:12-14)?

The parable of the sower can thus be read at two levels: it can speak about our fundamental attitude to the word of God; this, we should hope, is a response of faith and faithfulness. But the many sowings of the word in our daily lives may not be bearing much fruit. Hence the importance of emulating Mary's attitude toward the word.

But more is at stake than merely fruit in our personal lives. In his apostolic exhortation on devotion to Mary, Pope Paul VI asks that we adopt a contemplative attitude toward the world in the light of the word of God. After citing the two texts that show Mary pondering on the word of God (Luke 2:19, 51) he continues:

The church also acts in this way, especially in the liturgy, when with faith it listens, accepts, proclaims

and venerates the word of God, distributes it to the
faithful as the bread of life and in the light of that word
examines the signs of the times and interprets and lives
the events of history (*Marialis Cultus*, 17).

Charismatic renewal needs to be alert to its thrust toward the world: it cannot remain at the purely personal
level. The great Calvinist theologian Karl Barth once said
that the will of God is discerned by reading the Bible *and*
the newspapers. The Bible read out of our context will not
let the word reach fruition. The world on the other hand
needs to be confronted with the word of God. Hence the
importance of reading the Bible and the newspapers as
interrelated.

This poses the important question of how we are to
understand the Bible. To become a qualified biblical
scholar is the work of many years and most of us do not
have the opportunity for such study. The matter of the ac-
curacy of our reading of the sacred text must be raised. It is
of crucial importance to the charismatic renewal if only because there is such enthusiasm for the Bible within the
movement.

The common charismatic gift related to the Scriptures is
not easy to identify. It is not a substitute for exegesis: patient scientific study of the text is still needed. The charism
does not substitute for the work of scholarship, but it brings a
heightened awareness that this is God's word *to me*. The
words come alive, often with fresh meaning.

Technically, we are dealing here with two meanings of
Scripture. The first is what the human author intended.
This is called the *literal* meaning and this is the inspired
sense of the sacred text. The other meaning—namely,
what God says to me here and now through the text— is
called the *spiritual* meaning. Neither meaning alone is sufficient.

We have available in the church the results of the schol-
arly work that has been done over the centuries to arrive at
the literal meaning. Ideally this work of exegetes should be

aimed at teaching me more about the Scriptures, leading me to a deeper understanding of the text. At times scholars seem rather to be emasculating the text, more concerned to warn against traditional exaggerations than to build up the faith of the reader.

Charismatic renewal, nonetheless, needs to emphasize the literal meaning. Those who have some training in exegesis have a valuable contribution to make to prayer groups and other meetings in the movement. The danger is that there will be insufficient interest in the literal meaning, the inspired sense, and that enthusiasts will concentrate on the spiritual meaning, what God says to me here and now through the Scriptures.

It is not an exaggeration to say that it is the spiritual meaning that feeds the church in its life and liturgy. The Lectionary and the Liturgy of the Hours are, with the Missal, the main prayerbooks of the church in the West. These books, which are mostly scriptural texts, are put into the hands of laypersons, religious and clergy, most of whom have little or no training in scriptural exegesis. Even when there is a homily, there is seldom a detailed exposition of the scriptural texts, because the homily may be based on any part of the liturgy of the day (see General Instructions, Roman Missal, nn. 41,42).

Despite the church's encouragement to all to read the Scriptures frequently (see Vatican II: *Revelation*, 21–22), it is also true that very little help is given to them to grasp the literal meaning. The result is that in practice they concentrate on the spiritual meaning almost exclusively, even in using the official prayerbooks of the church.

We might take as an example the use of a text found in the Liturgy of the Hours, Jeremiah 29:11, 13, found in Prayer during the Day on Fridays in the early part of Advent. The passage reads:

> I know the plans I have for you, says the Lord, plans for welfare and not for evil, to give you a future and a hope. You will seek me and find me when you seek me with all your heart.

Almost all readers will take this as addressed to themselves. It is a consoling text that assures us that God has a plan for us, a plan that guarantees our future. This may refer to our present life or to the more important future, which is to be with God. And we are also told that when we seek God we will find him. Inasmuch as this text is used in the liturgy of Advent, we can see another meaning to it. It can be seen as referring to the coming of the Savior: this is the plan *par excellence,* and if we seek him we shall surely find him.

Because there is no further help given in the liturgical book, the person who is praying is apt to think only of such spiritual meanings. There is no help whatever in finding the literal meaning of the text. This meaning is quite complex and would never be suspected by the average reader of the Prayer of the Church.

In fact the text from Jeremiah comes from a letter that the prophet wrote to those who had already been exiled to Babylonia in the year 597. The main captivity would take place some ten years later, when Jerusalem fell. The text of the letter indicates that the exile will be long (Jer. 29:5–7) but the exile is meant to purify Israel and the letter contains the consoling passage that is used in the Church's Office.

The passage from Jeremiah may be taken as a typical instance of how the literal (inspired) meaning is missed by the ordinary reader. It poses the serious question of erroneous interpretations. This would seem to be particularly acute in the charismatic renewal where there is such an emphasis on Scripture. As we look to Mary we can approach a solution.

She is presented to us as pondering the word of God, as not understanding the saying and action of Jesus (see Luke 2:19, 50–51). There are many obscure passages in the Scriptures; we will not understand them at first, if indeed we *ever* understand them. But there is a difference between not understanding and being in error in one's interpretation. The possibility of wrong interpretation remains, but it is not significant for most readers of the Bible if they read it in the community. Mary read the Scriptures in her Jewish milieu. She understood it as a Jewess. She taught the Scriptures to the growing Jesus, so that as a boy his grasp of sacred Scripture was that of a young Jew, taught his religion by his mother.

The reason why we do not go astray in reading will be our contact with the community. We come, as members of the church, to hear the word of God. In our listening to the word addressed to us today we have in addition the light of the Spirit, his charism that enables us to appropriate the word as addressed to us. And this same Spirit will guide us into truth. Error will come if we set ourselves against the faith of the church, or if we are overhasty in accepting a particular interpretation as normative.

A knowledge of the literal meaning, the sense intended by the human author, will be a great protection for those who may have it. But this will not be the way for most, who will humbly ponder the word with submission to the faith they have already received. In this they will be truly marian in their approach. Emulating her questioning attitude of "how can this be?" (Luke 1:34), they will maintain a tranquil awareness of ignorance without any serious danger of being led astray.

On the principle that all the Scriptures speak to us of Christ, and many passages can be seen to teach us also about Mary, the *spiritual* meanings of the Bible are, nonetheless, also of value. The Old Testament looks to the New. Christ is the fulfillment of all that is hoped for: "All the promises find their fulfillment in him. That is why we utter the Amen through him to the glory of God" (2 Cor. 1:20).

The early church sought in Christ the full meaning of the inspired writings. Thus Peter uses Psalm 16, which is ascribed to David but written long after his time. It is a song of confidence; the author places his whole trust in the Lord. Peter sees this trust confirmed by the resurrection:

> I saw the Lord always before me, for he is at my right
> hand that I may not be shaken; therefore my heart was
> glad, and my tongue rejoiced; moreover my flesh will

dwell in hope. For thou wilt not abandon my soul in Hades, nor let thy holy one see corruption. Thou hast made known to me the ways of life; thou wilt make me full of gladness with thy presence (Acts 2:25; Ps. 16:8–11).

This Psalm speaks to us of the resurrection. But it also reflects the assumption: just as Mary had God ever before her, so he will preserve her from corruption. It may also be read as a song of our hope: we will not be left without help and support.

Mary is the perfect image of all that the church is to be (see Vatican II: *Liturgy*, 103). So we can take the teaching of Jesus and reflect on it in the spirit of Mary. She measures up to the demands of the sermon on the mount. She has achieved all that Paul wishes for the young churches: we can read the closing exhortations of his letters (e.g., Phil. 4; Rom. 12–16; Gal. 5; Col. 3–4; 1 Thess. 5; Eph. 4–5) and see the perfection of Mary in each one. They are a picture of Mary's life, of her relationship to God and to others because her "yes" to God was total. We might develop this from the conclusion of the First Letter to the Thessalonians. The text reads:

But we beseech you, brethren, to respect those who labor among you and are over you in the Lord and admonish you, and to esteem them very highly in love because of their work. Be at peace among yourselves. And we exhort you, brethren, admonish the idle, encourage the fainthearted, help the weak, be patient with them all. See that none of you repays evil for evil, but always seek to do good to one another and to all. Rejoice always, pray constantly, give thanks in all circumstances; for this is the will of God in Christ Jesus for you. Do not quench the Spirit, do not despise prophesying, but test everything; hold fast to what is good, abstain from every form of evil. May the God of peace himself sanctify you wholly; and may your spirit, soul and body be kept sound and blameless at the coming of our

Lord Jesus Christ. He who calls you is faithful, and he will do it.

This passage can lead to a rich marian meditation and one that provides important lessons for the charismatic renewal.

The first verses (12–13) call on the Thessalonians to respect those who are over them. We find Mary mentioned after the apostles in the Acts of the Apostles (1:13–14). It is Peter, not Mary, who takes an authoritative role in the task of replacing Judas (Acts 1:15). Again, it is Peter who addresses the crowd at pentecost (Acts 2:14). Mary is self-effacing before the leaders of the church. The charismatic renewal has its leaders, and they are to be respected. But we must look beyond the loose structures of the movement and be duly subject to church authority, esteeming highly those who are over us (1 Thess. 5:13).

There follows an exhortation to treat with gentleness and consideration those who are weak and to seek only the good (14–15). The picture that emerges of Mary in the New Testament is of one who is supportive, especially through prayer. There is no domination by Mary over others. In the charismatic renewal there is need for compassion, for the charism of encouragement. So many who come are wounded, weakened by sin, by a sense of failure and guilt. Even our greeting can, like Mary's (Luke 1:41), bring peace and a blessing.

The next section—on rejoicing, praying and giving thanks—reminds us of the Magnificat in which Mary is seen as rejoicing at God's wonders for his people and for her. She was told by the angel to rejoice, for the messianic times were at hand; she was to rejoice also as one receiving God's favor (Luke 1:28, 30). The joy of charismatic groups is something that strikes the outside observer. It is not a contrived emotion. To praise God is a decision. To sing a joyful song is not, primarily, a matter of feeling joyful but of recognizing the appropriateness of such a prayer.

To give thanks in all circumstances (see 1 Thess. 5:18) is

likewise a decision. The Lord's word to Mary was received with joy, but it was a word that would bring her sorrow. Her soul was to be pierced with a sword (Luke 2:35), she was to stand at the foot of the cross (John 19:25-27). To give thanks, to admire the plan of God, demanded on the part of Mary a profound commitment to his will. We are called upon to give thanks in all circumstances, not only in the relatively easy context of a prayer meeting.

The following verses (19-22) demand discerning judgment, prudence and faith. As we shall see later, Mary was docile to the Spirit and endowed with prophetic gifts. On the word of the angel she went to visit Elizabeth: this was a testing of the word of the angel both about herself and about Elizabeth. Charismatic renewal is open to the Spirit, but this must be tested again and again. And what is evil must be identified in order that we may abstain from it.

The passage ends with a commendation of the Lord's blessing of peace and an exhortation to constancy, for God is faithful (23-24). Mary's serenity is a trait that appears clearly in the Scriptures, except for the time when the boy Jesus was lost. *Then* she was anxious (Luke 2:45, 48). Because God is faithful we can be at peace in all circumstances. The only real worry is that we might lose God (see 1 Cor. 9:23-27; Phil. 2:12).

We conclude this chapter on Mary and the word of God by noting that the Scriptures show how Mary pondered God's word and she did not always understand it immediately. This makes Mary a model for us as we approach the Scriptures and hear God's word addressed to us. But these same Scriptures speak to us about Mary. We can find her attitudes, her mind, on practically every page of the New Testament, for she is the flawless model of everything the church hopes to achieve in its meditation on God's word.

The literal sense of Scripture retains its importance, for it is the inspired sense. But what will lead us closer to Mary, and hence to her Son, will be the new depths of the word that the Spirit continues to reveal to those who read the Bible humbly, with an "open and honest heart" (Luke 8:15).

Chapter VI

Mary and the Holy Spirit

POPE PAUL VI, in his apostolic exhortation *To Honor Mary*, encouraged us to reflect on the theme of Mary and the Holy Spirit (*Marialis Cultus*, 26–27). At first sight it may seem that the evidence for a developed theology of Mary and the Holy Spirit is slight. Nonetheless it is clear that there is such a theology, deeply rooted in the traditions of East and West. We shall examine the source of this theology in the Scriptures and show its development especially in the liturgy.

The incarnation is a work of the Holy Spirit in Mary. In St. Matthew's Gospel she is said to have been "found to be with child of the Holy Spirit" (1:18). Joseph's problem was what to do in this circumstance. Being a just man (Matt. 1:19), he was unwilling to act as if he were the father of this miraculously conceived child. (It is a completely unwarranted assumption that Mary never spoke to Joseph about the matter: he had a right to know.) Joseph does not know how to act justly.

The angel's message is reassuring for Joseph on precisely the point of being the putative father: he was to act as father and name the child Jesus (Matt. 1:21). It was the father's duty to name the child (Luke 1:62–63). If Joseph names the child, he then appears before the world as father. It is significant that Joseph is addressed as "son of David" rather than the more usual "son of Jacob" (see

Matt. 1:16), for it is through Joseph that Jesus enters the davidic line. Joseph obeys; he names the child Jesus.

This matthean text points to the central fact of Mary's relationship to the Spirit: she is mother of Jesus through the Spirit. St. Luke gives further insights into the mystery. In answer to her question "how can this be?," the angel replies: "The Holy Spirit will come upon you, and the power of the Most High will overshadow you; therefore the child to be born will be called holy, the Son of God" (Luke 1:35).

The expression "come upon" is a very special one for Luke. It is used in Acts 1:8 for the Holy Spirit's descent on the disciples at pentecost. It echoes the messianic prophecy of Isaiah 32:15, "until the spirit comes upon us from on high."

Parallelism is very common in biblical language: the same idea is expressed in slightly different terms in paired lines. In the lucan text above, we see that "the power of the Most High" in the second part of verse 35 is the same as "Holy Spirit" in the first part of the same verse. And Luke refers to the Spirit as power elsewhere. The disciples are told at the ascension, "stay in the city until you are clothed with power from on high" (24:49), an obvious reference to pentecost.

A key word in Luke 1:35 is "overshadow." This echoes the hovering of the creative spirit over the watery waste in the beginning (Gen. 1:3): the womb of Mary was likewise void, but would be made fruitful by the creative work of the Holy Spirit. More particularly, it evokes the cloud of God's glory that cast a shadow over the ark in the wilderness (see Exod. 40:35; Num. 9:18, 22).

Whether it was intended explicitly by Luke or not, we can see in this text a biblical background for the Litany of Loreto invocation "ark of the covenant." The ark was the sign of God's presence and power among his people. Mary through the power of the Spirit becomes the locus of Emmanuel, God-with-us. The word "overshadow" is also used in the account of the transfiguration (Luke 9:34).

The idea that Mary is the ark of the covenant emerges also if we can see the story of the transfer of the ark to Jerusalem in 2 Samuel 6 behind the account of the visitation. There are several similarities. King David leaps and dances (2 Sam. 6:16); the baby leapt in Elizabeth's womb (Luke 1:41). David says, "how can the ark of the Lord come to me?" (2 Sam. 6:9); Elizabeth says, "why is this granted to me that the mother of my Lord should come to me?" (Luke 1:43). The ark remains in the house of Obededom for three months, blessing its owner (2 Sam. 6:11); Mary remains with Elizabeth for about three months, having blessed Elizabeth and her unborn child (Luke 1:44, 56).

The liturgy of the East refers to Mary as ark of the covenant. On the feast of Moses (September 4) the church sings that the ark that he fashioned was to foreshadow Mary. On the feast of the annunciation the seventh canticle at Matins has the angel say:

> I see thee as a lamp with many lights and as a bridal chamber made by God. As an ark of gold, O spotless maiden, receive now the Giver of the law, who through thee has been pleased to deliver the corrupt nature of mankind.

The third significant element in Luke 1:35 is that Mary's Son "will be called holy, the Son of God." This will not be clear until after the resurrection. But it is a concern of St. Luke to show that the main lines of the gospel are present in the infancy account. We find a summary of salvation in the opening lines of the Epistle to the Romans. This may be a brief catechetical formula that Paul incorporates into the salutation of his letter. It is interesting to see that its three key notions are echoed by Luke in the annunciation account:

> *Romans:* the gospel concerning his Son descended from David according to the flesh (1:3) . . . and designated Son of God in power (1:4) . . . according to the Spirit of holiness (1:4).

Luke: the throne of his father David (1:32) . . . called holy, the Son of God (1:35) . . . the Holy Spirit (1:35).

What will be manifested later in power is already present in the annunciation in promise and partial realization.

The coming of the Spirit on Mary is to be seen in the light of Old Testament prophecies: the Spirit was to come on the branch of David (Isa. 11:2-4); the branch of the Lord will be holy (Isa. 4:2-3). These speak more of the coming of the Spirit upon the Messiah, which would occur at the baptism of Jesus (see Matt. 3:16 and parallels), rather than upon his mother.

Catholic tradition sees the preparation of Mary for the conception of her Son as a work of the Spirit: "the mother of God all holy and free from every stain of sin . . . fashioned by the Holy Spirit and formed as a new creature" (Vatican II: *Church*, 56).

The mother is prepared because her Son is the all-holy God. This preparation is the immaculate conception—preservation from all sin—and the gift of grace, both of which are works of the Spirit. She is as a result a "favored one" and she "found favor with God" (Luke 1:28, 30).

With the annunciation Mary enters into a new relationship with Persons of the Trinity. The three words of the angel reveal respectively the Father, Son and Spirit. And these lead to three corresponding reactions on the part of Mary. The first word telling her that she is favored and that God is with her provokes the feeling of fear. Before the glory of God the appropriate reaction is fear. Mary goes on to wonder about what the salutation means. The second word of the angel revealing her role in the birth of the Messiah and Lord leads her to ask how she is to act: "how can this be?" The third word is a revelation of the Spirit who will overshadow her. She now expresses perfect obedience, "I am the handmaid of the Lord."

Her reaction to the saying that the Lord is with her leads

to further revelation, which in turn culminates in the word about the Spirit. It is Mary's seeking of the path of obedience before God that marks this progressive revelation.

The church of the West sums up the trinitarian relationships in the liturgy of the annunciation:

> The Virgin Mary, receiving the angel's message in faith, conceived by the power of the Spirit and bore your Son in purest love (Preface, Roman Missal).

Mary's relationship to the Spirit grows throughout her life. It is through the Spirit guiding Simeon (Luke 2:25–27) that she learns more of the future destiny of her Son: he is salvation; he is light for the gentiles; he is the glory of his people (Luke 2:30–32). But he is also a sign to be spoken against (Luke 2:34).

Mary would be docile to the Spirit throughout her life. It is not hard to see in the Cana incident an exercise of strong, Spirit-filled faith. The account in John is to be taken along with Exodus 19. Both are divine manifestations (Exod. 19:16; John 1:51). They are on the third day (Exod. 19:16; John 2:1). The people accepts God's covenant, "everything the Lord has said, we will do" (Exod. 19:8); Mary points to a fulfillment of God's will, "whatever he says to you, do" (John 2:5). The glory of God is seen in each incident (Exod. 19:18–19; John 2:11). Mary can thus be seen as a perfect response to God's covenant love. She is the daughter of Sion, the embodiment of her people.

But there is more. She is addressed as "Woman." This looks back to the first woman, Eve (see Gen. 3:12ff) and looks forward to Calvary where she is again addressed as "Woman." Her constancy here was to be a crowning of the Spirit's gifts in her: her faith, hope and love were made perfect through tribulation (Rom. 5:3–5). She would later be in the upper room awaiting the coming of the Spirit, and she would receive a fresh outpouring of the Spirit (see Acts 2:4—"all" were filled).

There are many parallels between Luke 1–2, the story of

the infancy of Jesus, and Acts 1–2, the story of the infancy of the church. Both are primitive documents by the same author. They both look to major incidents in Israel's past to cast light on the present. We will return later to Acts 2. For the present it will suffice to note the more obvious similarities.

Both are in a closed environment: Nazareth, the home of Mary (Luke 1:28); the upper room (Acts 1:13). An outpouring of the Spirit is foretold in each (Luke 1:35; Acts 1:8). There is a sense of mission, of going forth, in both: Mary goes to Elizabeth (Luke 1:39); the disciples come out to the people in Jerusalem (Acts 2:1–6). There are outpourings of the Spirit giving rise to exultant praise (Luke 1:41–42; Acts 2:4, 11). Both books emphasize prayer and reflection (Luke 2:19, 51; Acts 1:14). Finally, the angel comes to Mary within the culture and religion of Judaism; it is from within the community of believers that Mary awaits the Spirit.

There is a last point to be made in regard to Mary's relationship to the Spirit. Just as Jesus' resurrection was a work of the Spirit (see Rom. 1:3–4), so the assumption is his final grace to her. The tradition of East and West is unanimous in assertions of Mary's being full of grace, always led by the Spirit, being his temple.

The Holy Spirit and Charismatic Renewal

Charismatic renewal knows the power of the Spirit. We have already noted his role in the manifestation of Jesus as Lord. Further, he constantly renews the church and leads it to more perfect union with its spouse (Vatican II: *Church*,4). The work of renewal of the church belongs to the Spirit. Individual renewal is likewise his gift; in charismatic renewal it is associated with baptism in the Holy Spirit.

We have already seen that, though this term is not without its difficulties, it can be used if we are clear that what is involved is not a new initiation, for there is only one baptism (see Eph. 4:5). We understand by baptism in the Holy Spirit a conversion that includes a fresh outpouring of the Holy Spirit. We can always be filled anew, if we avoid an overly material view of "filling." From the first moment of her conception Mary was filled with the Spirit, yet the Spirit could overshadow her at the annunciation, and she could be filled again at pentecost. This is because being filled means being loved more by God. Grace is the effect in us of the love of God that has been poured out into our hearts by the Holy Spirit (see Rom. 5:5). We can always receive more of God's love and hence we can be filled anew. In the eucharistic prayers of the Western church there is always a prayer for the Spirit to come upon the assembled people:

Let us be filled with every grace and blessing (I).

May all of us who share in the body and blood of Christ be brought together in unity by the Holy Spirit (II).

Grant that we who are nourished by his body and blood may be filled with his Holy Spirit and become one body, one Spirit in Christ (III).

By your Holy Spirit gather all who share this bread and wine into one body of Christ, a living sacrifice of praise (IV).

Likewise in the East we find similar prayers. Thus, for example, from the Liturgy of St. Basil:

We beseech and implore thee, O Holy of Holies, by the good will of thy goodness, for thy Holy Spirit to come upon us . . . . Unite us all that partake of the one bread and the chalice to one another in the communion of the one Holy Spirit

Mary was sinless and grace-filled from the first moment of her existence. Nonetheless, she received a fresh outpouring of the Holy Spirit at the annunciation and at pentecost.

In her relationship to the Spirit, Mary is our model. If Jesus is to be born in us, we too need to be overshadowed by the Holy Spirit. We need to be receptive and open to his action. When we allow him to touch us and make of us a new creation (see 2 Cor. 5:17; Gal. 6:15), we are in the obedient state of Mary, eager to receive. This involves continuous docility to the Spirit. The great work that he does within us is to make us adopted children of the Father, so that we too with Christ can cry "Abba, Father" (Rom. 8:14–15, 23).

We leave to the following chapter the consideration of the charisms of the Holy Spirit that were given to Mary and are present to the charismatic renewal. Our concern here is with the profound reality of the Spirit's work in the renewal. We find visible evidence of it in the lives that are changed, in the healings, spiritual as well as physical, and in the fruits of the Spirit that are manifest in so many persons (see Gal. 5:22–23).

What is important is that our attitude be truly marian, for the Mother of God said a "yes" to a relatively unknown future. Afterward the Spirit guided her. But it is noteworthy that Mary is led to divine truth also by other persons who themselves received revelation. It was to the shepherds, not to Mary, that the angels announced the birth of one who was saviour, Christ the Lord (Luke 2:10, 17). The old man Simeon was inspired by the Spirit and prophesied about the child and about Mary: her Son will be salvation, light, glory, a sign of contradiction, and Mary's own soul will be pierced (see Luke 2:30–35).

Charismatic renewal needs to be alert to the danger of an illuminism—that is, any tendency to prefer direct revelation to other means at arriving at truth. Mary was once directly enlightened by God, at other times indirectly. So in the charismatic renewal, though we know the power of the Spirit to guide us directly, we must also value his guidance through other persons, through the Scriptures, through the teaching of the church. Again, cases of distress and suffering do not need a charism such as prophecy to stir others to take action. Ordinary simple means and the gift of common sense are to be highly valued, even when the Spirit is pouring out other gifts.

Continuous prayer for the outpouring of the Spirit is needed if the Church is to come to fullness of life. He must overshadow the works of God's people that they may produce fruits of holiness and love. Prayer for the Holy Spirit is always answered. This we see in two significant passages, in Matthew and Luke. In the preaching of Jesus recorded in Matthew's account of the sermon on the mount we find the saying:

> If you then, who are evil, know how to give good gifts
> to your children, how much more will your Father who
> is in heaven give good things to those who ask him!
> (7:11).

But by the time that Luke came to write his Gospel the church knew the good thing *par excellence* that the Father gives, and so he records the saying as:

> If you then, who are evil, know how to give good gifts
> to your children, how much more will the heavenly
> Father give the Holy Spirit to those who ask him (11:13).

The Holy Spirit lies behind all the activity of charismatic renewal. It is through the love of God poured out by him into our hearts (Rom. 5:5) that we know we are loved. He is the Spirit of holiness (Rom. 1:4) who brings us into new life through faith (Gal. 3:2-5), and enables us to proclaim Jesus as Lord (1 Cor. 12:3). He is the Spirit who distributes charisms (1 Cor. 12:11). He is the power of mission in the church (Vatican II: *Missions*,4).

As we consider Mary and the Holy Spirit we can feel a double need: we are concious that we have to be taught about Mary and about the Holy Spirit. As the one who was most docile to the Spirit, we ask for the intercession of

Mary that we may learn more profoundly about his work in our lives. As mother of the church, she is concerned that the church come into fullness of truth about the Holy Spirit and through him.

At the same time we stand before the consoling mysteries of Mary: we are awed by the greatness of God's work in her. We can implore the guidance of the Spirit that our attitude and devotion to Mary be in line with the truth. We seek his light that we may avoid both exaggeration in her regard and excessive caution in celebrating what God has done for her.

Chapter VII

Mary and the Gifts of the Holy Spirit

MARY is not only an example for the whole church in the exercise of divine worship, but she is clearly a teacher of the spiritual life for individual Christians (*Marialis Cultus*, 21). This teaching of Pope Paul VI would encourage us to see Mary as teacher and model in that way to God and of serving the church that is the charismatic renewal.

Particular attention has to be given to the matter of the charisms of the Spirit. The charismatic renewal knows the power of these gifts. It knows wise use of the gifts as well as misuse of these very great benefits that God is bestowing on his church. It is important that we look to Mary as a model of how to relate to the gifts of the Spirit. We can also see her as one who was enriched with special charismatic gifts.

Wrong attitudes to the gifts of the Spirit can come about by either excess or defect. We err if we attach central importance to the gifts. But it is also a mistake not to be truly open to the gifts of God. The first error is to emphasize the gift rather than the Giver, to lose sight of the purpose for which the gifts are given—namely, the upbuilding of the church. The second false approach can reflect negligence in failing to avail of what God offers or, worse, a self-sufficiency that would deny the need of what God sees fit to give.

We return again to the necessity of a truly marian attitude: to be open to God's will, even without fully understanding what it may mean in concrete instances. We can look to Mary for a delicate balance in realtion to charism: we welcome God's gifts, but we do not overstress their role. At the center of our spirituality lies the affirmation "Jesus is Lord"; all else is subordinate.

With regard to the gifts of Mary, classical mariology often operated on the triple *potuit, decuit, fecit:* God could (give), it was appropriate that he (give), he did (give). This principle which goes back to Eadmer (d. ca. 1130), the disciple of St. Anselm, is not without merit, but it can be overused. In studying the charisms of Mary as well as her attitude to them, it is preferable to look to the Scripture and solid tradition rather than to deduce our conclusions from an abstract theological principle.

Mary and the Charism of Praise

The gift of praise is ascribed to Mary in the canticle of the Magnificat (Luke 1:46–55). We can leave to scholars the question of authorship: is it a song of the early church? Is it a composition of Luke? Is it the actual prayer of Mary? What is important to us is the fact that the word of God gives it to us as an appropriate prayer for the virgin of Nazareth.

It is a canticle of praise, a celebration of the marvels that God has done for his people and is now doing in Mary. As pure praise it is God-centered, the emphasis being not on Mary but on God. It is a song of the poor of Yahweh. In the Old Testament there was a grouping of persons called the *anawim*, the poor. They learned a profound trust in God: because they had no power, no wealth, no military strength, they turned to God in their weakness. They came to know him as the God who cares for the poor, who raises up those who depend only on him. The Magnificat firmly places Mary in this special category.

Praise is a gift that reaches out to eternity. We are to live forever in the praise of God. If this is to be complete blessedness for us, the perfection of our humanity, praise must answer the deepest needs of the human heart. It is not difficult to see why. The human heart is made for God: the innermost core of our being will find peace only in him (cf. St. Augustine's famous aphorism: "our hearts are made for you, and they will never find rest until they rest in you"). Praise is a reaching out toward God. It is a declaration of our creatureliness and a celebration of God's omnipotence.

In studying the Magnificat we can consider it as the song of the virgin of Nazareth: it reflects Mary's attitudes and spirituality at the time before the birth of her Son. But on a second level we can see it as an appropriate song of the queen of heaven: its sentiments have a permanent truth that applies to Mary now as well as when she walked this earth. At still another level we can apply it to ourselves: from very early times it has been the evening prayer of the church. When reciting the canticle we can be conscious of any one of these levels of meaning.

The structure of the Magnificat is that of many of the hymns of praise in the psalter—for example, Psalms 8, 19, 29, 33, 103. Like them it has an introduction praising God, a central section that gives reasons for praise, and a conclusion. There is some material in the Old Testament that is rather similar to the Magnificat, most notably the hymn of Hannah (1 Sam. 2:1–10), the hymns in Habukkuk 3:18f, and Isaiah 41:8–9. But the thought in the Magnificat is distinctly New Testament.

In the introduction God is celebrated as Savior: "My soul magnifies the Lord, and my spirit rejoices in God my Savior" (Luke 1:46–47).

The longings of her people are summed up in this opening praise. Like Judith (16:11) Mary sings a song of deliverance: the oppressed find their hope in God alone. The opening phrase can be seen as a commentary on the angelic salutation that Mary is receiving God's favor (Luke 1:28). Mary can praise the Lord continually. Her praise of God leads to her rejoicing.

Praise is not a matter of emotion, something that merely

expresses an exuberance, a joy in life. Fundamentally it will remain a decision: I decide that I will here and now praise God. The charism gives an added facility and so too does practice. The joy that praise engenders is not a matter of feeling or emotion: it is rather the sense of harmony, of peace and right relationship to God.

We can decide to praise God for his great deeds in Mary and use the Magnificat for so doing. We can also use Mary's hymn to praise God for what he has done in us. In both cases we praise a saving God; the Lord who kept Mary free from all sin is the same God who will set us free from sin and enable us to rejoice in him. Either considera-tion—namely, of God's work in Mary or in our-selves—will be a prayer that centers on God's loving and saving providence.

The central section of the hymn is in two parts, the first composed of 48–50:

> For he has regarded the low estate of his handmaiden.
> For behold, henceforth all generations will call me
>   blessed.
> For he who is mighty has done great things for me,
>   and holy is his name.
> And his mercy is on those who fear him
>   from generation to generation."

This first part celebrates God as mighty, holy, merciful. He is the savior God who loves his people. It is the God whom the people learned to trust even in poverty. Mary takes these covenant terms as motives for praising the power of God. His power is an important New Testament concept. Jesus would be "a man attested by mighty works" (Acts 2:22). The "power of the Most High overshadows" Mary (Luke 1:35). She was assured that nothing is outside God's power (Luke 1:37).

In the charismatic renewal the charism of praise is very common. There is in the movement as a whole a stress on this gift. Quite common is the giving of testimony, which is a faith-sharing of some grace or event in one's life. This comes from the motivation to praise God by acknowledging publicly what he has done, and also to lead others into praise. There can be less genuine testimony in which there is lack of sensitivity to the group present, bad taste or a failure to keep the mighty works of God to the foreground so that the emphasis is on the person giving testimony rather than on God. Mary looks to herself only to discover what God has done for her, and gives him praise.

Mary proclaims God to be holy. Jesus will later be called the "Holy One" (Acts. 3:14). Mary has already been told that her child will be called "Holy, the Son of God" (Luke 1:35). Praise needs to stress the holiness of God. The incarnation brings God near. The eternal Father is revealed as *Abba* ("Dad"; see Mark 14:36; Rom. 8:15; Gal. 4:6). But we need to keep the element of reverence in prayer: God is the Wholly Other, he is eternal, "he dwells in unapproachable light" (1 Tim. 6:16). Jesus calls us friends (John 15:14), but he is also Lord. Praise helps us to maintain balance in our prayer.

He is also merciful. The Hebrew word (*hesed*) in the background here is one of the commonest attributes of God in the Old Testament, especially in the Psalms. God is faithful to his promises, kind and merciful to his people. It is by reason of this quality that the sinner finds God approachable. The other two attributes—his power and his holiness—must be kept in mind, but it is in the context of God's mercy that the Christian penetrates them more fully. The Mighty One is kindly, the Holy One is faithful: these are the truths that lead God's people to praise him, serve him and fear him.

It is the realization of the mercy of God that gives us a correct fear, not a servile anxiety. This last is a fear of punishment, a fear of the evil that may befall us. The fear of God that is praised so often in Scripture is one that comes out of love and rests on an awareness of God's kindly compassion. It is a fear that does not forget that God is all-holy but nonetheless delights in his mercy. It is the fear of children who know they are loved and who love in return.

The second part of the central section of the hymn goes on to give further motives of praise:

> He has shown strength with his arm,
> he has scattered the proud in the imagination of their
>   hearts,
> he has put down the mighty from their thrones,
>   and exalted those of low degree;
> he has filled the hungry with good things,
>   and the rich he has sent empty away (Verses 51–53).

This passage singles out six great deeds of God on behalf of the poor and against the strong and rich. The Magnificat refers to them in the past tense. It does not stress that God had done these things in the Old Testament, as indeed he had, but that in Jesus there is a definitive statement on values: wealth and power are not important in the sight of God. Already with the incarnation of the Son of God in his humble handmaid (Luke 1:38) lowliness and poverty become special areas for God's favor. God has spoken his word about dominant values: "he scattered the proud . . . put down the mighty . . . sent the rich away empty." But he is the merciful, faithful God who loves the poor and so "he has shown strength . . . exalted those of low degree . . . filled the hungry".

The Magnificat concludes with a summary of God's relations with his people: "He has helped his servant Israel, in remembrance of his mercy, as he spoke to our fathers, to Abraham and to his posterity forever" (verses 54–55).

Again the mercy of God is stressed. It is in fulfillment of what he promised to Abraham that God sends the Messiah to the world. In the past he had indeed helped Israel (Verse 54); now his definitive help is seen. In the charismatic renewal we come to know the great and final word spoken by God to us in the Son (Heb. 1:2). We know the faithfulness of God to his covenant with us. We also know that God is continually making all things new (Rev. 21:5).

He helped his servant Israel in the past; he is still helping those who call upon him.

The canticle gives a spirituality of charism as well as an illustration of the particular charism of praise. It points to God who bestows gifts on his people, the One who is mighty, holy and merciful. It indicates how his people are to be before him: lowly, because he is mighty. Charism comes from God; its reception is a lesson in humility, for it is God who is acting. To receive charism with openness is to acknowledge that God's power is needed to fulfil his work. And the natural response to God at work in his world is praise.

Mary and the Charism of Intercession

As charismatic renewal matures, the charism of intercession develops. This is more than simple petition: it involves taking upon ourselves the weight of the needs of others in union with the great intercession of Christ (Heb. 7:25). It is a prayer that does indeed heal the intercessor, for it is a prayer that is totally unselfish.

One of the messianic prophecies was that there would be poured out on the house of David "a spirit of compassion and supplication" (Zech. 12:10). We look on the needs of the church and the world, and we raise our united prayer to God for them. In Mary we have a great intercessor and a model for our exercise of this very special prayer.

The church in its liturgy, which is the great teacher of prayer, does not normally pray to Mary directly, as if she had the power to answer our requests. Rather, the church prayerfully asks Mary to intercede, requesting her to take our needs upon herself and present them to the Lord. When the Roman Catholic Church calls Mary mediatrix and prays to her, this is what is meant. The church knows the text: "For there is one God, and there is one mediator between God and men, the man Christ Jesus" (1 Tim. 2:5).

Just as we have no difficulty in asking one another's

prayers, so in the Catholic tradition we feel that there is some special advantage in having Mary pray for us, she who is inseparably linked to her Son's saving work (see Vatican II: *Liturgy*,103).

The Hail Mary, the most common prayer to Mary, begins with praise of God's work in her and praise of her Son, the fruit of her womb, and then concludes: "Holy Mary, Mother of God, pray for us sinners now, and at the hour of our death."

But direct prayer to Mary is also found. The earliest marian prayer, the *Sub tuum praesidium*, may date from as early as the third century. In it we pray:

> We fly to thy patronage, O holy Mother of God. Despise not our petitions in our necessities, but ever deliver us from all danger, O glorious and blessed Virgin.

We can take as an example of mixed prayer one by Paul the Cenobite used in Compline in the Byzantine church. It asks for Mary's intercession, but it also addresses Mary directly for her help:

> O Lady, bride of God, virginal, pure, immaculate, blameless, without stain or disgrace, who through your birth-giving united God the Word with our human nature, and established a link between our fallen state and the things of heaven; O you, only hope of the hopeless, help of the oppressed, ready protection of those who flee to you and refuge of all Christians: despise me not who am a wretched sinner, who have defiled myself with unclean thoughts, words and deeds, and in my slothfulness have become a slave to the passions of life. Because you are the mother of God who loves all humankind, have mercy, have compassion on me a sinner and a prodigal son; accept this prayer from my impure lips, and, with the power of your maternity, beg your Son, my Lord and my God, that he may open

for me the depths of his loving kindness, forgive my countless sins, convert me to true repentance, and make me faithful to his commands. O you who are compassionate, be my constant companion: in this present life, be with me as an intercessor, as a powerful help to turn away the assaults of my enemies and to guide me to salvation; at the hour of my death, be with me to embrace my poor soul and to keep away the dreadful sight of the wicked devils; on the terrible day of judgment, deliver me from eternal punishment and make me an heir of your Son's glory, through the grace and the love for humankind of your Son our Lord and Savior Jesus Christ. To him and to his eternal Father and to his all-holy, good and life-giving Spirit we send up all glory, honor and worship, now and always and forever and ever. Amen.

In the life of Mary we note the power of her intercession at Cana. Yet her prayer was only a simple observation, "they have no wine" (John 2:3). Jesus' answer, as we have already seen, looks back to the woman of Genesis (2:23) and looks ahead to Calvary. At the foot of the cross the Beloved Disciple is first given to Mary as her son; only then is she given to him (John 19:26–27). She is to care for all the other disciples of her Son until the end of time. And indeed not only they, but all are her children and she is queen of all (Vatican II: *Church*,59).

The period between the ascension and pentecost was a time of fervent intercession. The apostles "with one accord devoted themselves to prayer, together with the women and Mary the mother of Jesus, and with his brethren" (Acts 1:14).

We might note in this text the phrase "with one accord." A key to the prayer of intercession is unity of mind. Even if we intercede alone, we must intercede with the mind of the church. If our prayer is with others, it is guaranteed an answer if we are gathered in the name of Jesus and are agreed about what we are asking (see Matt. 18:19–20). The picture in Acts is of united intercession with "Mary by her prayers imploring the gift of the Spirit who had already overshadowed her in the annunciation" (Vatican II: *Church*,59).

As the charism of intercession develops, charismatic renewal becomes conscious of the deeper needs of the church, which is always in need of renewal. Already by intercession we can enter into the task of renewal, for we act as the prophetic figure in Deutero-Isaiah:

> Upon your wall, O Jerusalem, I have set watchmen; all the day and all the night they shall never be silent. You who put the Lord in remembrance, take no rest, and give him no rest until he establishes Jerusalem and makes it a praise in the earth (Isa. 62:6–7).

From Mary we know the power of intercession. We ask her intercession. We model ourselves on her as we ask for the charism of intercession.

Mary and the Charism of Tongues

We have several times referred to the picture of Mary with the apostolic community united in prayer to "receive power" (see Acts 1:8 and 1:14). The answer to that prayer came on the day of pentecost. From the second century A.D., and possibly earlier, the Jews celebrated the giving of the law on that feast. Thus the Christian people celebrates the new law in the Spirit on the day that commemorates Sinai.

In the lucan narrative there are some similarities with the giving of the law in the Old Testament. On the mountain in the desert there was thunder and lightning, and the Lord descended in fire (Exod. 19:16, 18); in the one place where all the disciples were gathered there was:

> a sound from heaven like the rush of a mighty wind and

filled all the house where they were sitting. And there appeared to them tongues as of fire, distributed and resting on each one of them. And they were all filled with the Holy Spirit and began to speak in other tongues as the Spirit gave them utterance (Acts 2:2–4).

There are several points of contact here. In Jewish legend (not attested to in the Bible) it was said that when God spoke to Moses he spoke in many languages so that all the peoples might understand the law. Clearly too the story of the tower of Babel is behind the account in Acts: sin led to multiple languages and confusion (Gen. 11:1–9); the coming of the Spirit leads the citizens of many nations to understand the disciples.

The text in Acts is not without difficulties. Some initial questions arise. Why are the disciples accused of being filled with new wine (2:13) when it was not the wine season? This may alert us to a messianic new wine (see Mark 2:22; Matt. 26:29). Again, the charge of drunkenness would be strange if it were merely a matter of languages. In a city such as London or New York one continually hears strange languages—without assuming that the speakers are drunk. And Jerusalem was a very cosmopolitan city; foreign languages were commonplace.

These considerations have prompted many exegetes to surmise that what is involved here is a kind of ecstatic speech. The marvel, then, is not that diverse peoples heard or understood speeches in their own language but rather that in the confused babble all understood that there was praise of the mighty works of God (Acts 2:11). This enables us to grasp the meaning of the passage, though some difficulties do remain. The text in Acts is not an on-the-spot account, but a narrative composed many years afterward in a very stylized way. What we are asserting then is that the pentecost experience resembled the gift of tongues in First Corinthians.

The first gathering of the church in Acts 1:14 shows that the prayer for the outpouring of the Spirit was not confined to the leaders but extended to the disciples, among whom was Mary, given by Luke here the solemn title of "Mary the Mother of Jesus" (Acts 1:14). Then we are told that all were gathered in a house (Acts 2:1–2). The Spirit rested on each; all were filled with the Holy Spirit and began to speak with other tongues (Acts 2:4). This "all" includes Mary, who thus praised God in tongues.

If we are right in asserting that the pentecost event shows a gift of tongues similar to First Corinthians 14, then we can have more light from the modern phenomenon of glossolalia or tongues as experienced in the charismatic renewal. This gift is not one of specific languages, but, as we have already seen, nonrational sounds pronounced in faith and thus a vehicle of praise for the recipient. The speaker does not understand what he or she is saying (see 1 Cor. 14:14), but that is not necessarily a disadvantage, for we do not know how to pray as we ought (Rom. 8:26). We offer these utterances to the Spirit praying within us, so that he may draw "fine praise" from it (St. Augustine on singing in tongues).

The gift of tongues is primarily a gift for prayer (see 1 Cor. 14:14–17). There can be speech in tongues at an assembly, but it calls for the complimentary gift of interpretation (see 1 Cor. 14:13). Paul refers to singing in tongues in 1 Corinthians 14:15 and perhaps also in Colossians 3:16. This is well attested to later by St. Augustine, who calls it "jubilation":

> This is the way of singing God gives you; do not search for words. You cannot express in words the sentiments which please God: so praise him with your jubilant singing. This is fine praise of God when you sing with jubilation. You ask, what is singing in jubilation? It means to say that words are not enough to express what we are singing in our hearts. At the harvest in the vineyard, whenever men must labor hard, they begin with songs whose words express their joy. But when their joy brims over and words are not enough, they

abandon even this coherence and give themselves up to the sheer joy of singing. What is this jubilation, this exultant song? It is the melody that means our hearts are bursting with feelings words cannot express. And to whom does this jubilation belong? Surely to God who is unutterable (*In Ps. 32, Serm. 1, 8*).

We can look to the pentecost scene and to Mary to learn the appropriate use of the charism: it is to be as the Spirit gives utterance (see Acts 2:4). It is least among the gifts; Paul places it last in his list (1 Cor. 12:10). Nontheless, he values it and wishes that all the Corinthians prayed thus; it is an important, even if modest, gift (see 1 Cor. 14:5, 18).

Mary and the Charism of Prophecy

Mary is called "queen of prophets" in the Litany of Loreto. This is in virtue of her exaltation in the glory of the assumption and her reign in heaven, which has begun. But we can also look more closely at the Scripture and find in her an exercise of prophecy and a model for the charismatic renewal. We have already considered in outline the charism of prophecy when speaking about the role of faith in the gifts.

The basic meaning of prophecy is speaking for God. Prophecy covers the general fact that our life and words are to proclaim God. The word also has a more specific meaning—namely, what is spoken as a result of the inspiration of the Holy Spirit. We find both forms of the gift in Mary. Her whole life was a speaking for God. Her great *fiat* (Luke 1:38) would be lived out in a pilgrimage of faith that shows us the values of silence, withdrawal, emptying before God as well as before men and women. She lived in Nazareth, regarded by all as very ordinary (Matt. 13:55–57). This Nazareth life still speaks to the church: it underlines the value of the contemplative life; it consoles those who do not seem to have any major opportunity of serving God and others.

But Mary also spoke prophetically. Her words to the waiters at Cana after an apparent refusal by Jesus bear all the marks of prophetic inspiration. Jesus gives no sign that he will work a miracle, yet Mary is confident that he will help, and she says to the stewards, "Do whatever he tells you" (John 2:5). Inasmuch as her assurance did not come from the words of Jesus, it seem plausible to conclude that it came from an inner word, a prophetic impulse.

Her canticle is likewise prophetic. The parallel canticle in the first chapter of Luke is introduced by the words, "Zechariah was filled with the Holy Spirit and prophesied, saying . . ." (1:67). Mary too had been filled with the Holy Spirit. Her Magnificat begins with the Greek word *megalynei*, which is associated with tongues in Acts 10:46: "they spoke in tongues and magnified God." Tongues and prophecy are considered together also in Acts 19:6: the Holy Spirit came upon those on whom Paul laid hands, "and they spoke in tongues and prophesied."

This association of the two gifts occurs also at pentecost. Peter, from among those speaking in tongues, appeals to the text in Joel as being fulfilled on pentecost day: those they see are not drunk, "but this is what was spoken by the prophet Joel":

> And in the last days, it shall be, God declares,
> that I will pour out my Spirit on all flesh,
> and your sons and your daughters shall prophesy,
> and your young men shall see visions,
> and your old men shall dream dreams;
> yea, and on my menservants and my maidservants in those
>   days I will pour out my Spirit; and they shall prophesy
>   (Acts 2:16–18).

Ecstatic types of behavior were associated with prophesy in the Old Testament—for example, Numbers 11:25–29; 1 Samuel 10:6. This perhaps led to association of prophecy and tongues in Acts.

Mary's praise was prophetic, for prophecy is much more *forth*telling than *fore*telling. The Magnificat praises the divine plan as it has been revealed and as it is to be worked out. She celebrates the salvific mercy, God's covenant love for his people. It refers to the present and the future. In the special tense used in the Greek text, the aorist, there is already a sense of fulfillment. Mary will be called blessed by all generations (Luke 1:48). Old Testament expectations for the posterity of Abraham will all come about.

Thus we see in Mary a life that is prophetic, bearing witness to God and his plans. We also find prophetic utterances from her. In both ways she is paradigmatic for the charismatic renewal. It must alert Christians to the prophetic office of baptism and confirmation (see Vatican II: *Church*,35) and encourage expectancy for the charism of prophecy.

Prophecy is a gift of the Spirit and it will grow the more the Spirit comes upon (Luke 1:35) and fills (Acts 2:4) the bearer of the charism. The charism develops according as the recipient becomes ever more prompt and ready to speak the word of God and be seed on good soil (see Luke 8:15). All the time the prophet must draw others to the Lord, encouraging them, in the words of Mary, to "do whatever he tells you" (John 2:5).

The prophetic charism is given to the church to make it more sensitive to the word of God and consequently more obedient. To the persons gifted with prophecy and to those who hear them speak, there applies what was first spoken in praise of Mary, "Blessed rather are those who hear the word of God and keep it" (Luke 11:28).

Finally, we can point to the tradition of the western and eastern churches. In both we find the title "prophet" given to Mary. At times it is seen as a fulfillment of the text of Isaiah 8:3: "the prophetess conceived and bore a son." But more frequently it is the fruit of meditation on two texts of Luke: "the Holy Spirit will come upon you" (1:35) and her saying "all generations will call me blessed" (1:48).

Ancient writers who ascribe prophecy to Mary include Irenaeus (d. 202), Clement of Alexandria (d. 448), Ambrose (d. 397), Jerome (d. ca. 419), and many others, up to Albert the Great (d. 1193) and Thomas Aquinas (d.1274).

Mary and the Charism of Healing

We have already spoken of Mary as the perfectly healed one: always sinless, she never knew the emotional and spiritual scarring of sin. From his mother Jesus was to receive perfect humanity untouched by any contamination coming from ancestral sinfulness. He took our sinful condition freely upon himself: "he was made to be sin, who knew not sin" (2 Cor. 5:21). This was in fulfillment of the servant prophecy: "He was wounded for our transgressions, he was bruised for our iniquities . . . with his stripes we are healed . . . the Lord laid upon him the iniquity of us all" (Isa. 53:4-6).

The First Letter of Peter echoes this text, showing that our healing comes from the sinless one: "He committed no sin; no guile was found in his lips . . . He himself bore our sins in his body on the tree that we might die to sin and live to righteousness. By his wounds you have been healed" (2:22-24).

It was in virtue of the merits of her Son who was to die for her as well as for the rest of humanity that Mary was kept free from all stain of sin. On the Cross Jesus suffered for the gift of the immaculate conception that Mary had received.

Mary is not only fully healed and thus a "a sign of hope and comfort" (Preface of the assumption, Roman rite), she is invoked in the Western church as "health of the sick . . . comforter of the afflicted" (Litany of Loreto). In Scripture and tradition we find this strongly emphasized. For St. Ephrem (d. 373) she is "the healing of untreatable wounds" (*Orat. ad Dei Matrem*). In the fathers and early writers sometimes the main emphasis in the visitation story is on the greeting of Mary, sometimes on the unborn Jesus' touching his unborn precursor. Doubtless both are intended in the lucan narrative.

The unborn John is described as leaping in his mother's womb at Mary's greeting (Luke 1:41). This is a fulfillment of the angel's word to Zechariah, "he will be filled with the

Holy Spirit even from his mother's womb" (Luke 1:15). This is clearly a divine action beyond the power of any creature. Origen (d. ca.254) argues that through the divine presence in Mary's womb there was healing from the wounds of soul and body (*Hom. VII in Luc.*). Elsewhere Origen and Ambrose stress the miracle worked by the un-born Jesus.

A fifth-century Greek homily of uncertain authorship develops in some detail the incident with major stress on Mary:

> Then she went with haste to the house of Zechariah and, imitating the angel, saluted Elizabeth. When Elizabeth heard the greeting of Mary the child jumped for joy in her womb and Elizabeth was filled with the Holy Spirit. The voice of Mary was efficacious and filled Elizabeth with the Holy Spirit; through her voice and prophecy as by a perpetual fountain she sent a river of charisms on her cousin. This caused dancing and exultation in the feet of the infant still bound in the womb. This was a sign and symbol of a miraculous religious dance. When, indeed, fullness of grace appears all things are filled with joy (P.G. 10, 1166).

There is another healing grace through Mary in the New Testament that we can barely glimpse and speculate upon. In the gathering of the early church there is Mary's forgiveness of the apostles who had abandoned her Son. Having shared his hours on Calvary she can mediate his forgiveness.

The modern charismatic renewal knows of powerful gifts of healing given by the Spirit of Jesus to the church. There are those to whom this gift is given in great abun-dance. Others flock to such persons and this is understand-able. Prayer for healing is common wherever we encounter the charismatic renewal. But we need to be more alert to healing gifts that are less spectacular in the life of the church.

There is healing in love, healing in forgiveness, healing in being made welcome, healing in greetings. The empowering of the Holy Spirit in John the Baptist and his mother Elizabeth at the greeting of Mary can sensitize us to the wide range of the Spirit's healing work and protect us from an interest in healing that is centered on gifted persons rather than on the Lord who heals. Everyone can be a minister of healing and of compassion to the weak and the burdened.

Both eastern and western liturgies stress the healing power of the Eucharist. Thus in the Liturgy of St. John Chrysostom the priest prays:

> Not unto my judgment, nor unto my condemnation, be the participation of thy holy mysteries, O Lord, but unto healing of both soul and body.

Similar is a prayer from the Roman liturgy:

> Lord Jesus Christ, with faith in your love and mercy I eat your flesh and drink your blood. Let it not bring me condemnation, but health in mind and body.

In each Mass we pray, "say but the word and I shall be healed." It is worth recalling here the theological opinion given prominence by the French Jesuit Maurice de la Taille—namely, that the dynamism of the early church was due in no small measure to the presence of Mary at eucharistic celebrations. The power of her intercession brought innumerable blessings on the apostolic church. This would encourage us to stress intercession for spiritual and bodily health in the Mass. The power of God is there to heal: we need to believe in this power and evoke it to bring his gifts, including healing, upon the church. A ministry of healing centered on the Eucharist will certainly be fruitful, if less striking.

We need in this matter to adopt a marian attitude to the power of the Lord: while accepting the charism of healing as a great benefit, we know that the Lord is not bound to work within the area of charism. Nonetheless, as the charisms were powerful and fruitful in the early church through Mary's intercession, we need to imitate her earthly prayer and be joined to her heavenly petitions that we be healers and be healed.

In our times we know that persons are healed through the intercession of Mary. The great shrines, such as Lourdes, Fatima and Knock, are centers of healing. One of the great values of so many marian shrines is that they alert us to God's will to heal the sick and the broken. This is not to say that all are *cured* in the restricted sense that their sickness is taken away, though undoubtedly there are many such restorations to health. Healing is something broader than curing. One might say that most pilgrims are healed in Lourdes but not all are cured. They are touched by God through the prayers of the Virgin Mary.

This continuing role of healing through the mother of God can teach the charismatic renewal to have profound faith in the healing power of God. There is no situation so hopeless that God's love cannot ameliorate it. Every instance of illness—physical, emotional, spiritual—can be brought in faith to the Lord that the healing he wishes for the person may take place. We need to learn, as Mary learned, "with God nothing will be impossible" (Luke 1:37).

Mary, Charismatic

It may seem tendentious to refer to Mary as charismatic. Yet the evidence shows it to be true: she exercised what we have learned to call charisms and she is our model in so doing. The charismatic renewal, with its heightened awareness of charism, can indeed see more in the texts of Scripture than has been customary until now. New things and old must be continually brought out of the church's treasury (see Matt. 13:52).

One apparently new feature of the charismatic renewal is the raising of hands and arms during prayer. Yet this is as old as the church. We read in the First Letter to Timothy: "I desire that in every place the men should pray, lifting holy hands without anger or quarreling" (2:8).

In paintings of Mary the earliest in the catecombs show her in the *orans* position, arms raised and spread out. This classical pose would last for centuries and enter the Eastern icon tradition.

We can always return to the picture of Mary in the Scriptures and as elaborated in tradition to learn how we are to follow her Son within the charismatic renewal. As herself a bearer of charism she teaches the church that all of us must "earnestly seek the spiritual gifts" (1 Cor. 14:1) and be "eager for the manifestations of the Spirit"(1 Cor. 14:12).

Chapter VIII

Mary and Mission

THE VATICAN II Constitution on the Church has a striking passage on Mary and the apostolate. It was added at a late stage in the preparation of the document, at the instigation of Cardinal Suenens:

> The church, therefore, in its apostolic work too, rightly looks to her who gave birth to Christ, who was thus conceived of the Holy Spirit and born of a virgin, in order that through the church he could be born and increase in the hearts of the faithful. In her life the virgin has been a model of that motherly love with which all who join in the church's apostolic mission for the regeneration of humankind should be animated (n. 65).

The church is missionary of its very nature (Vatican II: *Missions*, 2). In its continual outreach it has Mary as its model. The section of the Constitution on the Church quoted above shows at what precise point Mary is to be regarded as model of the church's apostolic activity: specifically as mother of Christ. She gave birth to him, and the church likewise brings him to birth and to increase in the heart of the faithful.

This emerges clearly on close examination of a text of Mark's Gospel:

> A crowd was sitting about him; and they said to him, "Your mother and your brethren are outside asking for

you." And he replied, "Who are my mother and my
brethren?" And looking around on those who sat about
him, he said, "Here are my mother and my brethren!
Whoever does the will of God is my brother, and sister,
and mother" (3:32–35).

At one level this seems a simple incident in the public life of
Jesus: his family is looking for him. He uses the occasion to
stress that "doing the will of God" is far more important
than family bonds. The disciples listening to him "are" his
mother and brethren. As we saw in the analysis of the
greeting of Elizabeth and the incident of the woman in the
crowd (Luke 11:27–28), Mary is blessed above all by her
faith: she is more fortunate in being the woman of faith
than in being the mother of the Lord.

But there is another level at which we can consider the
passage in Mark. It becomes clearer if we separate the
"brother/sister" from the "mother" relationships. First, then,
"whoever does the will of God is my brother and sister." In
doing the will of God we become more his children. The
Father and the Son come to us (John 14:23). As our relationship with the Father grows deeper, so too does our
relationship with the Son. As we become more and more
children of God, we also become more and more brothers
and sisters of Jesus. This might be thought of as the vertical
pole of Christian existence: relationships with God the
Father through the Son in whom we abide (see John
15:6–10).

Now we turn to the second part: "whoever does the will
of God is ... my mother." A mother brings forth a child
and cares for it. As we do the will of God, we give birth to
Jesus in our surroundings. We cause him to be present in a
way in which he was not hitherto. We allow him to grow
and increase in others. "Doing the will of God" reflects the
maternity of Mary who brought forth Jesus and nurtured
him. This might be seen as the horizontal pole of our existence: as we serve God, we touch our neighbors, for we
bring them Christ, we cause him to be born or to increase
in their midst.

The rich meaning of the marcan text emerges in other places in the New Testament. Mary is seen several times as presenting Jesus. The shepherds found Mary, Joseph and the baby (Luke 2:16). This is put in a still more striking way by Matthew: "going into the house (the Wise Men) saw the child with Mary his mother" (2:11). Mary brings Jesus to the temple with Joseph (Luke 2:22) so that the aged Simeon may acknowledge his savior and the salvation of all peoples (Luke 2:30–32). Anna, the prophetess, recognized in the child brought by Mary the One who would redeem Jerusalem (Luke 2:38).

We have already examined in some detail the visitation story. Here we can take the key ideas and focus them around the idea of mission. Mary goes to care for her elderly cousin. But she is also concerned to see the fulfillment of the sign given to her (see Luke 1:36). She is not to know as she sets out that she was the instrument chosen to implement the prophecy given by the angel to Zechariah, that his son would be filled with the Holy Spirit from his mother's womb (Luke 1:15, 41). Mary takes the one step indicated and God's plans are furthered. She goes as the ark of the covenant, for in her is a new presence of God to his people. The glory of God hidden in her brings a blessing on the house of Elizabeth.

Mission and Charismatic Renewal

We can see Mary as model for mission by comparing the visitation story with the incident of the healing of the lame man in Acts. Peter says to the cripple at the Beautiful Gate: "I have no silver and gold, but I give you what I have" (Acts 3:6). Peter, in the name of Jesus, gave healing to the man. Mary brings Jesus to the house of Elizabeth. The particular mission of the charismatic renewal in the church is to give what it receives.

The initial experience of individuals who encounter the renewal—for example, at a prayer meetings—is often "we have found the Lord" (see John 1:41). This should lead to the baptism in the Holy Spirit, to new conversion, to the reception of charisms. But it cannot remain at this stage. Andrew's reaction on meeting Jesus was to go and tell his brother Simon Peter and bring him to Jesus (John 1:40–42). Charismatic renewal knows the lordship of Jesus and the blessing this is. It must then be outreaching, passing on to others what is received.

A charge frequently made against the charismatic renewal is that it can be too inward-looking, too vertical, in its thrust and not sufficiently concerned with urgent social questions. One can answer such criticism by noting that, although the charismatic renewal as such does not take up specific issues and is not committed structurally to institutions of caring, nonetheless those involved in the renewal are to be found engaged in charitable and social works. One of the fruits of the baptism in the Holy Spirit is the freedom from selfishness that allows more concern for one's neighbor.

But there is a more profound answer. Even though each individual in the renewal is called upon to be more loving and caring, the most fundamental call to the movement in the church is not to social action but to evangelization. This is the work of spreading the good news that we have received. "I give you what I have" then becomes a message about having met a loving Lord, a saving God. It is not so much telling others about Jesus as putting them in living personal contact with God. This is evangelization. It is more than catechesis, which normally should follow and is an explanation of the doctrines that surround the Christ-event.

Evangelization received a major impetus after the synod of bishops had requested Pope Paul to issue a major document on the topic. This he did in 1975 with the magnificent apostolic exhortation, *Evangelii Nuntiandi*, which he issued on the feast of the immaculate conception. He concludes it with a section on "Mary the Star of Evangelization":

It is with joy that we confide our desires to the Blessed

Virgin Mary on this day specially consecrated to her immaculate conception and the tenth anniversary of the
close of the Second Vatican Council. On the morning of
pentecost she presided in prayer at the beginning of
evangelization under the guidance of the Holy Spirit.
May she shine forth as the star of that constantly renewed
evangelization that the church, in obedience to the com-
mand of the Lord, must promote and accomplish especially in these days, so difficult but so full of hope.

Mary is the model for evangelization in being fully
docile to the Holy Spirit. In a major section of the exhortation, Paul VI insists on the need for the Holy Spirit to be
present and active in each evangelizer. Techniques of evangelization are excellent, but without the Holy Spirit the
most convincing dialectic has no power over the human
heart.

Called to evangelization, the charismatic renewal will
take part in this mission in the way that is characteristic of
it. It will be according to the way in which the Holy Spirit
has guided it from its beginnings in the church. For the renewal, evangelization will center on baptism in the Holy
Spirit through which persons come into close personal love
of the Savior. For the many blockages to an acceptance of
God's love, the movement will be sensitive to the healing
gifts of the Lord given to his people. Healing will be offered
to individuals in the sacraments, through healing prayer,
in loving encounters in which each finds acceptance and
genuine caring. The fruit of evangelization will be praise of
the Father and a new depth of prayer in the one evangelized.

Other groups in the church will evangelize in other
ways, with a differing emphasis. The spirituality of the
charismatic renewal, especially as seen in the Life in the
Spirit seminars, will determine the particular evangelistic
approach to be taken. As with other aspects of its life, in
this too Mary will at every stage be the exemplar.

The concerns of this chapter can be seen in summary
form in a passage from St. Augustine in which he com-
pares Mary and the church:

The church is therefore a virgin. It is, and may it remain a virgin: let it beware of the seducer who would lead it to corruption. A virgin is the church. You might say to me, if it is a virgin, how does it bring forth children? And if it does not bring forth children, how have we taken its name as being born from its womb? I would answer: it is a virgin and it does give birth. It imitates Mary who gave birth to the Lord. Did not Mary give birth and remain a virgin? Thus the church gives birth and is a virgin. And when you think of it, it gives birth to Christ, for it is his members who are baptized. "You are," the apostle says, "the body of Christ and its members" (1 Cor. 12:27). If the church gives birth to the members of Christ, it is most like Mary (*Tract. de Symbolo*, 7).

As in each other area we have been considering, Mary is not only model of what the church wishes to achieve (Vatican II: *Liturgy*, 103), but she is also the intercessor that this may be accomplished. The Second Vatican Council ends its document on the Missionary Activity of the Church by referring to Mary as queen of apostles. This traditional invocation of the Litany of Loreto takes on a new appropriateness in this time when the charismatic renewal, along with the whole church, is to be rededicated to the apostolate to all humankind.

These ideas can be found in a fine summary in the liturgy of the Western church:

Almighty Father of our Lord Jesus Christ, you have revealed the beauty of your power by exalting the lowly virgin of Nazareth and making her the mother of our Savior. May the prayers of this woman clothed with the sun bring Jesus to the waiting world and fill the void of incompletion with the presence of her child (Prayer from the vigil of the assumption).

Chapter IX

Mary and the Family of Her Son

IN CHARISMATIC RENEWAL we can find a new understanding of one of the concluding articles of the Apostles' Creed: "I believe . . . in the communion of saints." From its first insertion into the creed in the fourth century this affirmation was understood to refer to a communion—that is, a sharing—both of holy persons and of holy things. The Greek and the Latin originals of the creed can be translated either way. Rather than adopt one version the church has tended to take both meanings, even though at various times it may have stressed the sharing in holy things more than the fellowship with holy persons, as seems to be more the case nowadays.

The Eastern Orthodox churches and the Roman Catholic Church have emphasized the communion of saints more than have the various Protestant churches. In their hymns, their prayers, and above all in their icons, the churches of the East are continually conscious of the family of God, especially in the celebration of the liturgy. The Roman Catholic Church is mindful of the three stages of the church: the church triumphant in heaven, the church suffering in purgatory, the church militant still struggling on earth.

Charismatic Renewal and the Communion of Saints

The most obvious aspect of the communion of saints seen in the charismatic renewal is the sharing of holy things. We see persons caring for one another through prayer and intercession and in practical ways of loving. The gifts of renewal are for others. There is profound sharing in faith experience as persons tell how they encounter the living God and know his love in the events of their lives. The sharing of the word of God is a very special instance of faith sharing, and through it we build one another up in holiness. This sharing is not only with those whom we find congenial: to be authentic it must have the character of Christian love, and thus be open to whomsoever God may send to us.

As the charismatic renewal becomes more mature there is a thrust toward community. There are many styles of this in the worldwide phenomenon of the charismatic renewal, but each takes its inspiration from the early church in which the members of the Jerusalem community "dedicated themselves to the apostles' teaching and fellowship, to the breaking of bread and the prayers" (Acts 2:42).

This text and some others in Acts (see 2:43–47; 4:32–37; 5:12–16) have from earliest times been the source of community in the church. Religious communities, basic ecclesial communities and many other movements in the church today apart from the charismatic renewal movement all look to these texts as a permanent fount of light and guidance.

It will be helpful to consider the four elements in the text quoted above. We come together in community on the basis of the apostles' preaching. It is not from preference or from pleasant association or mere friendship that we build community; rather it is on the foundation of the death and resurrection of the Lord and his new commandment to love one another as he loved us (John 13:34): this is why we give ourselves to one another.

The simple prayer meeting too has community dimensions even though they are neither very demanding nor very rich in expression in many places. There is, as we have said, caring and sharing of what we have received. And there is seriousness in following the apostolic preaching as received in our church.

The third element of community follows from the first two: from obedience to the apostolic instruction we can share in the breaking of bread. Our unity in community is most profound in the Eucharist: "because there is one bread, we who are many are one body, for we all partake of the one bread" (1 Cor. 10:17).

The common sharing of the Eucharist builds community. Where this is not possible in interdenominational communities or prayer meetings, we can only seek deep love for our fellow Christians in the individual participation of the Lord's Supper: I take part in the Eucharist carrying my separated brothers and sisters in my heart. In the teaching of the Vatican Council the Eucharist is the "source and apex of the whole Christian life" (Vatican II: *Priests*,5).

Because the Eucharist contains Christ and we encounter him in it, we are at the same time closest to our brothers and sisters when we are united with our Lord. From our sharing in the Lord's supper we come to fidelity to prayer. We need to pray together and to pray alone if we are to become strong enough to love one another. We need regular prayer to discover the will of God and to be wise (see Eph. 5:15-17). Prayer alone is not enough. In a sense its fruit follows the other three elements of the primitive Jerusalem community. They pursued the apostolic teaching; they had common or shared life; thus their eucharistic sharing was authentic. From this they could have a profound prayer life.

Growth in community is slow, it is lifelong. We need the support of others if we are to follow Christ. In turn, we must share our riches, our strength, with others. In this growing alongside one another there will be need for continuous healing of all the emotional and spiritual scars that flaw our mature development.

Indeed, in the communion of saints we find a new understanding of purgatory, as we have already noted. Rather than consider it as a place of punishment, we should more properly see it as a state of healing, of the final healing before the vision of God. And just as we can help to heal others with our prayer, so our intercession can have power beyond the grave to bring healing to those in need (see 2 Macc. 12:43–45). This is what lies behind the Roman Catholic doctrine on purgatory.

Our efforts to establish community in the charismatic renewal and elsewhere does not depend solely on our own efforts. We are involved in a wider reality that includes the whole family of God. Our labor in caring, in sharing, in loving is under the affectionate eyes of our friends in heaven. What we are seeking to build is but a pale image of what they already enjoy. What is at issue here is not merely the veneration of the saints but of life alongside and with them. The Second Vatican Council states:

> The authentic cult of the saints does not consist so much in a multiplicity of external acts, but rather in a more intense practice of our love, whereby, for our own greater good and that of the church, we seek from the saints' example in their way of life, fellowship in their communion and the help of their intercession (*Church*,51).

In this family life of God we have Mary as queen and mother. Along with the Roman Catholic Church, the Orthodox churches do not hesitate to call Mary queen: she is exalted above all in heaven, next only to her Son. She is also mother. She is mother of the whole Christ, head and members. She gave birth to the Son of God. On Calvary the Beloved Disciple was given to her as son. In his first encyclical, Pope John Paul II notes that from then on:

> All generations of disciples, of those who confess and love Christ, like the apostle John, spiritually took this mother into their own homes (John 19:27) (*Redemptor Hominis*, 22).

In the communion of saints Mary is mother, but she is also model. She entered fully into the Father's plan: "God so loved the world that he gave his only Son" (John 3:16). She gave up that Son on Calvary. She continues to give him, not now unto death, but for our sanctification.

The motherhood of Mary in our regard is well explained by the Second Vatican Council:

> This motherhood of Mary in the order of grace continues uninterruptedly from the consent that she loyally gave at the annunciation and that she sustained without wavering beneath the cross, until the final fulfillment of all the elect. Taken up into heaven she did not lay aside this saving office but by her manifold intercession continues to bring us the gifts of eternal salvation. By her maternal charity, she cares for the brothers and sisters of her Son, who still journey on earth surrounded by dangers and difficulties until they are led into their blessed home (*Church*, 62).

What is here stated in austere theological terms is found more poetically in the Matins of the assumption in the Orthodox church:

> O Mother of God, thou living and plentiful fount, give strength to those united in spiritual fellowship, who sing hymns of praise to thee. In thy divine glory vouchsafe unto them crowns of glory. O pure Virgin, sprung from mortal loins, thine end was conformable to nature: but because thou hast borne the true Life, thou hast departed to dwell with divine Life Himself.

An authentic attitude to Mary will not be content with devotions. It is the experience of persons involved in the charismatic renewal that they develop a new love for well established devotions such as the Rosary and the Angelus. As the Scriptures come alive, as a regular prayer becomes established, new values are seen in many traditional practices. But full piety toward Mary recognizes her as model, as mother, as one who loves and cares.

Our reflections on the communion of saints give confidence as we seek to build community, which is the maturest fruit of the charismatic renewal to date. We share holy things, we share life with holy persons living and dead, but alive in Christ. In doubt and failure we have always a mother and queen.

As so often before, we can turn to the liturgy to find our deepest thoughts expressed. In this prayer of the Roman liturgy, from the Mass of the assumption, we find the heart of all that charismatic renewal hopes for:

> Father in heaven,
> all creation rightly gives you praise,
> for all life and all holiness come from you.
> In the plan of your wisdom
> she who bore Christ in her womb
> was raised body and soul to be with him in heaven.
> May we follow her example in reflecting your holiness
> and join in her hymn of endless life and praise.